FUNDAMENTALS OF
Tibetan Buddhism

by

Rebecca McClen Novick

Copyright © 1999 by Rebecca McClen Novick

All rights reserved. Published in the United States by Crossing Press, an imprint of the Crown Publishing Group, a division of Random House, Inc., New York.
www.crownpublishing.com
www.tenspeed.com

Crossing Press and the Crossing Press colophon are registered trademarks of Random House, Inc.

Cover artwork of Shakyamuni Buddha courtesy of Bill Kane

Library of Congress Cataloging-in-Publication Data
Novick, Rebecca McClen.
      Fundamentals of Tibetan Buddhism / by Rebecca McClen Novick.
        p. cm.
   Includes bibliographical references.
   1. Buddhism — China — Tibet. 2. Tibet (China) — Religion.
 I. Title.
 BQ7604 .N68   1999
 294.3'923—DC21

                                  98-49025
                                     CIP

ISBN-13: 978-0-89594-953-0

Printed in the United States of America

Cover design by Courtnay Perry

15   14   13   12   11   10   9

First Edition

This book is dedicated to the
nuns, monks, and people of Tibet
who continue to be persecuted for their beliefs.

I am deeply grateful to Geshe Tsultim Gyeltsen for his radiant example, to all the teachers of the Tibetan Buddhist tradition for making their wisdom available, and to Lotsawa Tenzin Dorjee for his unwavering generosity of time and knowledge. Thanks is also due to Ven. Thubten Chödrön, Jesse Fenton, and John Jackson for sharing their superior knowledge of Dharma. Any errors in this book are mine, not theirs. I am also grateful to Bill Kane, to everyone at The Crossing Press for their support and to my husband, Ronny, for his love, patience, humor, and cooking throughout this project.

Contents

When the Iron Bird flies and horses run
on wheels,
the Tibetan people will be scattered like ants
across the world.

—EIGHTH CENTURY TIBETAN PROPHECY

My first contact with Tibetan Buddhists was as an interviewer working in the Tibetan refugee communities of Northern India. I was recording testimonies of torture and brutality in Chinese-run prisons in Tibet. The survivors I spoke with displayed an uncanny ability to come to terms with the agonies they had experienced. Their suffering was undeniable, and yet neither were they vengeful nor were their spirits broken. They remained radiant and resilient, often even expressing compassion for their oppressors. What was their secret? They answered again and again, "It was my faith in Buddhism."

A true test of any spiritual practice must be whether it can help you in times of crisis. It was clear from the Tibetans with whom I spoke that their worldview provides a perspective from which a deep and holistic understanding of existence, with its joys and its sufferings, can be built. For Tibetan Buddhists, daily life is an aspect of spiritual practice rather than the other way around—as is so often the case in Western society, and it is both inspiring and challenging to experience a culture in which the highest ambition is to become a human embodiment of compassion and the highest vocation is to develop the necessary wisdom to achieve this.

This book does not attempt to be a comprehensive guide, for Tibetan Buddhism is a vast and multifaceted arena (the Buddhist canon from which Tibetan Buddhism evolved is larger than the *Encyclopedia Brittanica*). I have, however, attempted to cover the fundamentals of this system within the limits of my understanding, in a straightforward and informative manner as a foundation for further study. Ironically, the treasure of Tibetan Buddhism has come into our hands because it is being destroyed in its homeland. The Chinese occupation of Tibet has caused a spiritual diaspora of Tibetan Buddhist teachings around the planet. In these times, we have an unprecedented opportunity to learn from this tradition, and whichever spiritual path we ultimately follow, I believe that we will forever be richer for having done so.

Introduction

My religion is loving kindness.

—DALAI LAMA **XIV**

In Tibetan, the word for Buddhist means "insider"—someone who looks not to the world but to themselves for the source of peace and happiness. The purpose of Buddhism is to relieve suffering; it begins with the premise that all suffering, however real it may seem, is the product of our own minds. Buddhism offers a remedy for every spiritual ailment. In fact, the language of medicine is often used in Buddhist scriptures as a metaphor for the spiritual journey: The spiritual mentor is the doctor, the practitioner is the patient, the negative mental and emotional states are the illnesses, and the antidotes to those conditions are the teachings.

Tibetan Buddhism is a way of experiencing the world, more than it is a religion or a philosophy. The Buddha did not teach a theory describing the universe; he taught a method—a prescription—for how to live in it. These teachings entice us to give up our defense against change. They inspire us to realize a completely courageous approach to life, without divine authorities, without even familiar psychological concepts of self-identity, and from that point of fearlessness to reach out to those still caught in the web of suffering. The Tibetan form of Buddhism goes a step further than the more ascetic schools, which emphasize a denial of worldly experience. It allows for a person to get completely involved in human affairs—in family, politics, art, and business—while fostering a fundamental awareness that it is all cosmic theater. Being free from the world illusion allows one to act freely in it. Tibetan Buddhism is, therefore, an attractive and sympathetic path for those who have chosen not to enter monastic life but to remain in the world to pursue their spiritual goals.

The historical Buddha, Shakyamuni, has taken on divine properties in Tibetan Buddhism, and serves as a template for the boundlessness of humanity's spiritual potential. This potential for Buddhahood is said to lie within every one of us. The Dalai Lama says that it is "something we have always had, from time without beginning....We are not talking about something completely foreign to our nature, which might suddenly appear like a mushroom, as though without seed or cause." There are no limits; everything is possible once we fully recognize and comprehend at the deepest level who we truly are. A Buddha is nothing less than a living realization of this understanding.

Such thinking might seem like an impossible dream, because presently we are the product of deeply ingrained habits that have become reinforced, say the teachings, through lifetimes of imprinting and social conditioning. It is only when we attempt to escape this mechanical behavior that we realize how trapped we have become. Buddhism offers a way out—a way that begins with our own awareness of our captivity and the desire to be free. Buddhism is like a hologram. Each part eventually leads one to the realization of the whole. Through whatever door you approach the teachings, whether it be impermanence, compassion, emptiness, or the karmic law of cause and effect, you will ultimately arrive at the same place, for each aspect of the teachings is just one facet of an integrated and interdependent understanding of oneself and one's place in the universe. Buddhism is highly evolutionary, offering the possibility for everyone to completely transform themselves—the "evolutionary momentum" in this case being one's own aspiration for Enlightenment.

Buddhists believe in the principles of love and compassion, but they do not believe in a creator god. In fact, questions as to how the universe was created and whether or not it is eternal are considered unimportant. Instead, the Buddhist attempts to answer the more immediate questions of how to overcome the problems and difficulties of life. Someone who spends time on such questions while ignoring spiritual practice is compared to a person who refuses to let a doctor pull an arrow out of his or her body until s/he knows everything about the person who shot it.

No one path suits everyone, and so there are practices for every kind of person. The Dharma (the teachings of Buddhism) adapts to the individual character and aptitude of the practitioner. The Dalai Lama has said that the Dharma can be practiced without conflict by Christians, Moslems, Jews, and Hindus. When the Buddha's disciples asked him how people would be able to differentiate between their master's words and the words of another after he was gone, he replied, "Whatever is well spoken is the word of the Buddha." In other words, if a teaching leads in the direction of lasting peace and happiness, then it has value no matter what its origin. This, plus the Buddha's refusal to appoint a successor, paved the way for a variety of interpretations of Buddhist doctrine, leading to a tradition of lively debate and an integral ability to adapt to changing circumstances. It also reflects Buddhism's highly pragmatic and nondogmatic approach, which generates not only a tolerance of but a respect for other spiritual traditions.

Buddhism has evolved through twenty-five hundred years of debate, inquiry, and analysis. The history of Buddhism can be seen as the history of a philosophical dialogue between teachers and students—a dialogue that is still going on today. The mind is seen as a vast laboratory, and Buddhist literature is full of experiments. Critical inquiry is considered indispensable, and personal experience the final test of truth. We should not accept the teachings merely on faith. The Buddha said,

"Just like examining gold in order to know its quality, you should put my words to the test. A wise person does not accept them merely out of respect." The Sutras (the discourses of the historical Buddha) speak of the "four reliances":

Do not rely on individuals, rely on the teachings.
Do not rely on the words, rely on the meaning.
Do not rely on the adapted meaning,
   rely on the ultimate meaning.
Do not rely on intellectual knowledge, rely on wisdom.

There is a Tibetan story about Gampopa, the founder of the Kagyu school. He was a monk and a doctor who became a disciple of the poet-saint Milarepa. Gampopa spent all his time meditating in a cave. One day, Milarepa asked him what he experienced during his meditations. Gampopa replied that he experienced nothing—only a great void. Milarepa exclaimed that if this were the case then the monk had not understood the teachings and was not truly meditating at all! Gampopa was so disillusioned that he decided to forgo his monastic robes and dress like Milarepa. Once again, Milarepa chastised him, declaring that copying others was not the answer. "Everyone must follow their own path. Heal yourself, good physician monk; then you will naturally heal others. My teaching is mine; yours must be yours. Do whatever is necessary in order to evoke it from within."

Origins of Tibetan Buddhism

Whether a Buddha appears or does not appear,
the true nature of things remains forever.

—PRAJNAPARAMITA SUTRA

The origins of Tibetan Buddhism are found in India. The historical Buddha was the son of a Hindu king who ruled a region of Nepal around the sixth century B.C.E. He was not the first *Buddha*, nor will he be the last. According to tradition, he is the fourth Buddha of this eon, and there are still 996 to come. The Buddha is known by a number of different names: Gautama, Siddhartha, and Shakyamuni. Gautama was his family name, and this was the title that most people of the time would have used, whereas the name his parents gave him was Siddhartha, which means "one who reaches his goal." Shakya was the clan to which the Buddha's family belonged. *Muni* means "sage," and in Tibetan Buddhism the Buddha is most often referred to as Shakyamuni, or "the Sage of the Shakyas." The Buddha before his *Enlightenment* is usually referred to as Siddhartha, and after his Enlightenment as the Buddha, a term that he used to describe himself that simply means "awake."

As a young prince, Siddhartha enjoyed a life of endless luxury. His father was so protective of him that he arranged life at the palace so that his son would never have to lay eyes on anyone who was not young, healthy, and beautiful. Thus, Siddhartha grew up knowing nothing of sickness, old age, or even of death. When he accidentally discovered these realities of life at the age of twenty-nine, he realized how little he understood about life and resolved to leave the palace and become a *Saddhu,* a homeless seeker of truth. Siddhartha studied with a number of great meditation masters and gained high levels of spiritual realization, but he always felt that he had more to learn. For many years, he lived as an ascetic, surviving on a few grains of rice a day. When, in spite of these extreme practices, he found that he was no closer to realization, he decided to stop denying his body and find a more balanced path to Enlightenment, a *Middle Way.*

Siddhartha sat down under a pipal tree (known as the *Bodhi*—"Enlightenment"—tree) and there he meditated for three days and three nights. He underwent all manner of spiritual trials and endured the doubts and mockery of his ego, but eventually he attained complete Enlightenment and became a

Buddha. At first, he was reluctant to teach, thinking that the path to realization could not be communicated so that ordinary people could understand it. The texts say that the gods Indra and Brahma came down to plead with him to turn the *Wheel of Dharma,* to teach what he had learned, and finally he acquiesced.

The Buddha expounded a total of eighty-four thousand different sections of teachings, to offer many different kinds of individuals the means for attaining Enlightenment. As much ink as an elephant can carry on its back is said to have been used to write the texts contained within each section. The three great teachings that the Buddha expounded are referred to as the "three turnings of the wheel of Dharma." The first "turning," or teaching, that the Buddha gave occurred at Varanasi (formerly Benares) in Northern India. Here he gave instructions on the Four Noble Truths, common to both the *Hinayana* and *Mahayana* schools of Buddhism. The second turning of the wheel of Dharma took place at Rajagriha, where the Buddha gave his teachings on emptiness: The *Prajnaparamita* ("perfection of wisdom") *Sutra,* which is a central document of Mahayana Buddhism, records these teachings. The third turning was given at Shravasti and covers teachings concerning the qualities of Buddhas. These three teachings are collectively called the *Sutras* and refer to the discourses that the Buddha gave directly to his disciples after his Enlightenment.

Around 200 B.C.E., texts appeared claiming to be the word of the Buddha. They were separated into three divisions and became known as the *Tripitaka,* or the "three baskets," and they make up the entire Buddhist canon. The Sutras were guides to meditation practices. The *Vinaya* were teachings that the Buddha gave regarding ethics and monastic discipline, and the *Abhidharma* texts deal principally with wisdom and with the nature of reality. Practitioners committed spiritual teachings to memory, as this was thought to inspire a more profound understanding than learning from written texts. Thus, everything in Buddhism is taught in sets of numbers: the *Four Noble Truths,* the *Six Perfections*, and so on.

After the Buddha's death at the age of eighty, Buddhism began gradually to spread throughout Asia. The great Indian emperor, Ashoka, widely encouraged it's dissemination, and, due to the seminomadic nature of Buddhist monastics, the Buddha's teaching soon found its way to new lands. The origins of Mahayana (the school to which Tibetan Buddhism belongs) are very obscure, but scholars agree that the Mahayana scriptures date from approximately 100 B.C.E–500 C.E. It was the great Indian philosopher, Nagarjuna, who founded the Madhyamaka, or Middle Way, school of Buddhism and established a framework for the Mahayana teachings of emptiness and the path of the *Bodhisattva*—a person who is traveling the path to full *Buddhahood.*

Buddhism in Tibet

There were three most kind to Tibet:
the Precious Guru, Padmasambhava;
the Lord Master, Atisha; and Precious Master,
Tsong Khapa.

—TIBETAN SAYING

Buddhism in Tibet has a history that spans more than a thousand years. The trade routes of Asia skirted Tibet's mountains, never penetrating her natural barriers, and for centuries the country remained largely isolated from the rest of the world. Little is known about Bon, Tibet's indigenous pre-Buddhist religion. Many scholars suggest that it was originally shamanic in nature, and indeed its magical and animistic practices and the ritual use of human bones suggest shamanic influence. Bon still survives today and has been reinterpreted within a Buddhist framework.

Tibetans view the history of Tibet as the story of how the Buddhist Dharma tamed their country's primitive energies. In a Tibetan myth, the land of Tibet rose above the waters of the ocean (an event that actually took place forty million years ago when the Indian subcontinent collided with Asia). The only inhabitants were a monkey and an ogress. The monkey, who was an incarnation of Avalokiteshvara, the Buddha of compassion, was a peaceful being and enjoyed meditating by himself in his cave. The ogress, on the other hand, had a wild and passionate nature. She had no idea that the monkey existed, and she desperately desired a companion. When, from the silence of his cave, the monkey heard her howls of loneliness, he felt enormous compassion for her and agreed to become her mate. This unlikely couple became Tibet's Adam and Eve. They had six children together, and it was from them that the entire population of Tibet descended. The ogress and the monkey are said to symbolize the conflicting character traits of the Tibetans themselves, who throughout history have been both aggressive and peaceful.

By the sixth century, Tibet began to develop militarily. At this point in history, the country was completely surrounded by Buddhist nations. These became the focus of raids by Tibetan fighters, who were known as the "red faces" because of their custom of using war paint made from red ochre. Under the leadership of the emperor, Songtsen Gampo, Tibet became a powerful empire that lasted for two hundred years. The "red faces" conquered vast regions of Central Asia between Tibet and China, and were considered such a threat that the rulers of the Chinese and Ottoman Empires united to try to halt the Tibetan expansion.

In 635 C.E., Tibet attacked China and later annexed Nepal. Songtsen Gampo married both a Chinese and a Nepalese princess from his conquered lands. These women, who were later regarded as incarnations of the goddess Tara—the emanation of all the Buddhas' wisdom and compassion who is often called the "mother of the Buddhas." The princesses were both devout Buddhists and brought Buddhist ideas and images from their homelands. Their influence on the king, and through him Tibetan society, largely inspired the spread of the Dharma in Central Asia.

While Europe was plunged into the cultural turmoil of the "Dark Ages," Tibet was undergoing a renaissance. It was the thirty-eighth Tibetan King, Trisong Detsen (740–798 C.E.), who established Buddhism as the state religion. The king was an enthusiastic convert to the new philosophy, and he asked the Indian tantric yogi, Padmasambhava, to come to Tibet to give teachings. Padmasambhava was a dynamic and charismatic character who is said to have possessed superhuman powers. He wandered the Tibetan countryside, subjugating the local demons and deities, instructing the local people and converting them to Buddhism. Together with Trisong Detsen, he founded the first Tibetan monastery at Samye, where he supervised the early translations of the Buddha's teachings from Sanskrit into Tibetan.

Later, around the middle of the ninth century, the great conqueror king, Relbachen, continued to spread the Buddhist faith throughout the land. During his reign, the great spiritual exchange that began with Padmasambhava reached new heights. Many Indian scholars came to Tibet to help translate Buddhist texts, and Tibetans went to India to study Buddhism. Relbachen was murdered by his ministers, who replaced the king with his brother, Lang Darma, an ardent supporter of the old Bon religion. Lang Darma destroyed Buddhist scriptures, closed down monasteries, and forced the monks to marry. He was eventually assassinated, but before his death he had almost succeeded in wiping out Buddhism from Tibet. The mighty Tibetan empire collapsed into chaos as tribal conflicts led to instability and separatism, and China was able to take back the areas it had lost. Tibet did not unite around a common leadership again for another three hundred years.

The second dissemination of Buddhism in Tibet was brought about by Yeshe Ö, a monk-king who ruled a western region of the country. In 1042, he invited the renowned Buddhist scholar, Atisha, to Tibet. Atisha had a profound impact on Tibetan society. He reformed the monasteries and emphasized the mentor-student relationship of lamas and disciples. He was dearly beloved by the general population, who embraced his teachings, and by the end of his career Buddhism was firmly established in Tibet. Dawa Norbu writes, "Perhaps no religion in the world has changed a people's way of life so dramatically as Buddhism did in Tibet. The Tibetans, who had been the most dreaded and fiercest warriors in Central Asia, literally 'put down their weapons at the lotus feet of lamas' and followed the 'white path of peace' pointed to by the Buddha."

Indigenous Buddhist schools emerged as Tibetans began to interpret the dharma in slightly different ways. Four of these schools survive today: the *Nyingma,* founded by Padmasambhava, the *Kagyu,* the *Sakya,* and the *Gelug* (see Chapter 20). In the twelfth century, Genghis Khan led Mongolia to a position of total dominance in Central Asia. In the middle of the thirteenth century, the Mongolian army invaded and overran the militarily vulnerable Tibet. In 1244 C.E., the Mongolian warlord Prince Godan, grandson of Genghis Khan, invited the head of the Sakya school, Sakya Pandita, to his camp. Sakya Pandita was a legendary and learned lama reputed to be the holiest monk in Tibet, and when Godan met him, the prince was so impressed that he converted to Buddhism. This marked the beginning of the extraordinary priest-patron relationship between the two countries, where Mongolia offered military protection in exchange for Tibet's spiritual knowledge. However, although the Mongols were nominally the rulers of Tibet, they left the day-to-day affairs of the country to the Tibetan people.

In 1253, Sakya Pandita's nephew, Pagpa, became the spiritual teacher of Kublai Khan, who installed him as the ruler of Tibet. Kublai Khan later became the Mongol emperor of China and declared Buddhism the state religion of Mongolia. The Tibetan lamas and Mongol khans continued their close relationship, but by 1307 the Mongols had lost much of their interest in Tibet, which was rife with internecine conflicts. Sakya power began to wane, and the country again fell to the rule of Tibetan warlords. Mongol power too began to decline, and in 1368, China was in a position to overthrow the Mongolian dynasty.

Around 1400, Tsong Khapa spearheaded a renaissance of Buddhism in Tibet and founded the Gelug school, whose name means "system of virtue." This school, known as the "Yellow Hats," became extremely popular in Mongolia as well as in Tibet. In 1578, a profound event occurred in Tibetan history, when Sonam Gyatso, the second reincarnation of Tsong Khapa's main disciple, visited the court of the Mongol ruler, Alta Khan. Echoing the auspicious meeting three hundred years earlier between Prince Godan and Sakya Pandita, the monk's demeanor, learning, and spiritual accomplishment deeply moved the great khan. He became a Buddhist and bestowed the title "Dalai"—the Mongolian word for ocean— on Sonam Gyatso, as a gesture acknowledging the depth of the lama's knowledge. Thus the priest-patron relationship was reestablished and the institution of Dalai Lama was created.

Sonam Gyatso is known as the Third Dalai Lama, as his previous two incarnations (Gendun Gyatso and Gendun Druba) were given the title posthumously. The Fourth Dalai Lama came from Alta Khan's own family, and this cemented the relationship between the two countries. By the end of the sixteenth century, Tibetan warlords had become increasingly defensive against the rise of monastic power, and they began a period of religious persecution. The Mongols came to the aid of the monastics and, buoyed by huge popular support, the Fourth Dalai Lama became the political as well as spiritual leader of Tibet.

The "Great Fifth" founded a government in 1642, and became the first Dalai Lama to lead a united Tibet. He wrote numerous books, mastered the tantric arts, and was a powerful ruler. He abolished serfdom by dismantling the private forces of the nobility and revoking their rights to determine the fates of the peasantry, who were at that time no better off than the medieval serfs of Europe. While monastic power in Northern Europe was dwindling and its military was on the rise, in Tibet the opposite was true. Tibet was the only place in the world where religious leaders gained hegemony over the military. The first Manchu emperor invited the Fifth Dalai Lama to his palace; he became, as did many subsequent Dalai Lamas, the spiritual guide to the Chinese leaders. As Tibet stabilized, it began to shut itself off from the countries surrounding it, and for three hundred years an uninterrupted succession of Dalai

Lamas ruled peacefully in Tibet. China, which now ruled Mongolia, left Tibet more or less alone, only interfering in periods of civil tension. The religious landscape in Central Asia had completely reversed, and Tibet was now the only Buddhist nation in the region.

TIBET IN THE TWENTIETH CENTURY

The Thirteenth Dalai Lama (1876–1933) was an exceptional man and a great ruler. He laid plans to bring Tibet into the modern era: to build roads, to improve the educational system, to reform the monasteries (some of which had become corrupt), and to bolster Tibet's military defenses. In some areas he was successful, but he came up against an intransigent conservative lobby that blocked many of his proposals. In 1903, a British expedition arrived in Tibet to forge a trade agreement that fully exploited the Tibetan government's economic naiveté. Seeing how easy it was for a foreign power to march into the capital, the Chinese general Chao Erh-feng began organizing a number of brutal raids into Tibet. His plan was to annex the country and capture its leader, but the Thirteenth Dalai Lama got wind of his plan and fled to India. Chao proclaimed that he had removed the Dalai Lama as the head of the country, but the Tibetan people ignored him and continued to view the Thirteenth as their leader.

As the Nationalists gained power in China, Chao lost his support, and the Tibetan government banished all Chinese officials and soldiers from its soil. However, when the Chinese Nationalists took political control of China, they began to recognize Tibet's strategic significance and its vast mineral wealth. Tibet's right to self-rule had not been questioned for more than three hundred years, but in 1912, the new Chinese leaders began claiming historical rights over their neighbor. In 1933, the Thirteenth Dalai Lama died, but not before he had prophesied the imminent destruction of his country.

The Thirteenth had foretold that he would be reborn in Eastern Tibet, and the search began for his reincarnation. In 1937, the ruling regent, Reting Rinpoche, in a sacred lake named Lhamo Lhatso, saw visions revealing the house where he would find Tibet's new leader. Following various signs and portents, Reting Rinpoche and his party found a house in the northeastern province of Amdo that matched the vision he had seen. The officials disguised themselves as merchants and began to question the two-year-old son of the family who lived there. The boy passed a number of intricate tests designed to determine if he was really the Thirteenth's true incarnation. The state oracles confirmed the discovery, and in 1940, at the age of four, the boy was enthroned as the new Dalai Lama.

By 1948, the Chinese leadership had fallen to Communist control, and the new government began publicly to question

Tibetan sovereignty. Once again, suspicious of their intentions, the Tibetan government expelled Chinese officials from the country. Tibet's fears were realized when on New Year's Day, 1950, Peking Radio reported its intention to "liberate" Tibet from Western imperialists, even though there were only six Westerners known to be living in Tibet at the time. At five million strong, China's army was almost the size of the entire Tibetan population. Due to the pressing circumstances, the government decided to officially inaugurate the sixteen-year-old Dalai Lama earlier than was customary.

After gaining control of the East, the Communists marched on Lhasa in 1951. By 1959, the country was suffering brutally under the Chinese rule. Torture was endemic; thousands of people were executed; *struggle sessions* (interrogations involving physical torture, psychological bullying, and public humiliation) were conducted in towns and villages to encourage Tibetans to turn against their neighbors; monks and nuns were forced to copulate in public; children were forced to shoot their parents. The violence could not have been a sharper contrast to the peace that had existed previously in Tibet. Before the invasion, about one-sixth of the male population of Tibet were monks, and almost every family had either a son or a daughter who had taken the monastic vows. (Although monks far outnumbered nuns, there were between six hundred and eight hundred nunneries in Tibet before the invasion.)

The monastic system allowed for a person from the humblest of origins to attain a privileged position through merit rather than birthright, but it was a system so utterly foreign to the communists (who despised all religion) that they could see it only as an example of feudalism with the monastics as overlords. If the Chinese found the Tibetan system incomprehensible, the Chinese Communist ideology was equally foreign to the Tibetans and contradicted the values they had held sacred for a thousand years. The young Dalai Lama tried to mediate and negotiate but to no avail. In his autobiography, he describes his inner struggle during this difficult time:

Only the thought of my responsibility to the six million Tibetans kept me going. That and my faith. Early every morning, as I sat in prayer in my room before the ancient altar with its clutter of statuettes standing in silent benediction, I concentrated hard on developing compassion for all sentient beings. I reminded myself constantly of the Buddha's teaching that our enemy is in a sense our greatest teacher. And if this was sometimes hard to do, I never really doubted that it was so.

On March 10, 1959, thirty thousand people swarmed around the Dalai Lama's summer palace to thwart what they suspected was a Chinese plot to kidnap their leader. Disguised as a soldier, the Dalai Lama fled to India to establish his government in exile. With their beloved spiritual leader gone, the monasteries and nunneries reduced to rubble, thousands of people dead and imprisoned, and the rest in grief and shock, Tibetan independence came to an end. China proclaimed that it had successfully annihilated the "darkest feudal serfdom in the world."

Mahayana

All these diverse systems are worthy of respect,
since they all have the potential to bring about
great benefit to a large number of
sentient beings.

—**DALAI LAMA XIV**

Mahayana is one of the two main *yanas* or "vehicles" of Tibetan Buddhism, the other being Hinayana. (In Tibet these two vehicles, plus the Tantric vehicle of *Vajrayana*, which incorporates the main aspects of both, were preserved and practiced.) The evolution of Mahayana as distinct from Hinayana was a very gradual one. With the growing popularity of the idea of the Bodhisattva—a person who evolves from an ordinary condition to that of a Buddha—the lay practitioner gained in status, and the monastics were no longer the sole spiritual heirs to the Buddhist tradition. The path of the Bodhisattva spans all

Buddhist traditions, but Mahayana emphasized this path above all others and developed it into the ultimate religious goal (see Chapter 14). By the time Buddhism reached Tibet, Mahayana had become an established and vital movement with its own texts and practices and a unique spiritual character.

Theravada, the only surviving school of Hinayana, is the most widespread form of Buddhism in the world and is dominant in the countries of Southeast Asia, such as Burma, Thailand, Cambodia, Laos, Vietnam, and Sri Lanka. Mahayana Buddhism is practiced in East and Central Asia in countries such as Korea and Mongolia, and also in China, Japan, and Tibet. Tibetans refer to Hinayana as the *Individual Vehicle* and to Mahayana as the *Universal Vehicle.* In Hinayana there are two subvehicles, *Hearers* and *Solitary Realizers.* The Hearers are those who gain *Liberation* from listening to the teachings of buddhas; Solitary Realizers are more advanced individuals who, in their last life before *Liberation*, attain this state independent of a Buddha's direct influence. The goal of the followers of the Individual Vehicle is to become an *Arhat,* a "foe-destroyer," one who has destroyed the enemy of delusion. Such a person gains liberation from cyclic existence and attains the peace of nirvana. This *Liberation* is not complete *Buddhahood,* however, which Mahayana teachings say can only be attained by following the path of the bodhisattva. Full Buddhahood is attained when one has eliminated the extremely subtle influences and imprints in one's psyche that cause a dualistic view of reality—one that perceives a distinction between subject and object and that misapprehend all things as possessing independent and inherent existence. It is characterized by a condition of omniscient *wisdom*, wherein all phenomena can be simultaneously and directly perceived, and all obstructions to knowledge are overcome. Mahayanists emphasize altruism, and the liberation of others is their main objective. They regard their path as more inclusive than that of the Individual Vehicle, offering religious practices for the layperson as well as for the monastic.

Unlike followers of Mahayana, Theravadins do not regard the Mahayana Sutras as the words of the Buddha himself, but as those of later interpreters of his teachings. They also believe that the Buddha encouraged individual Liberation rather than universal responsibility. It is wrong to assume, however, that followers of the Individual Vehicle are not altruistic. Arhats are said to possess extraordinary means to help others, but this is not their central purpose. Theravadins acknowledge and respect the spiritual ideal of the Bodhisattva, but they feel that only a limited number of extraordinary individuals can achieve it. They suggest that because the journey to full Buddhahood is so arduous and difficult (taking three "countless eons" to complete—a period of time so vast that it is akin to infinity) that most people should content themselves with pursuing their own personal salvations. Mahayanists, on the other hand, set themselves the infinite task. They claim that the seed of Buddhahood lies within each creature and that there is no fundamental difference between the Buddha and other people, or even other sentient beings such as animals and insects. Mahayana Buddhism emphasizes the presence and possibility of Buddhahood, but Theravadins believe that we will see no living Buddhas for another few millennia.

The "Perfection of Wisdom" Sutras, which appeared around 200 C.E., are the earliest Mahayana texts. In these texts, it is the Bodhisattva (rather than the Hearer or Solitary Realizer) who is presented as the spiritual role model. This literature also expounds upon the doctrine of *emptiness* as the ultimate nature of all reality. In Mahayana, the person of the Buddha is viewed as a superhuman figure who is not bound by the common laws of nature. Even his death is said to have been merely appearance, carried out as a teaching on the impermanence of phenomena, and the Buddha is believed still to reside in another dimension of reality, continuing to intervene in people's lives.

Followers of Mahayana regard their path as more complete than that of Theravada in its motivation, its ultimate aim, and the degree of understanding that it can inspire. However, Mahayana scriptures often caution the reader against disparaging Hinayana. In fact, one of the Bodhisattva vows is never to denigrate the Hinayana path. The Individual Vehicle is, after all, the foundation for the Universal Vehicle, and a Mahayanist must study and practice it fully. The great Tibetan meditation master, Dilgo Khyentse Rinpoche, said that it was better "to follow the outward model of Theravada Buddhism, inwardly to have the altruistic motivation of a Bodhisattva, and secretly to practice the vehicle of *Tantra*. That way all three vehicles become a single path."

The Four Noble Truths

Suffering must be recognized, and its origin
  eliminated;
and the cessation of suffering must be actualized,
and the path to cessation realized.

—DALAI LAMA XIV

The Four Noble Truths were the first teaching that the Buddha gave after his Enlightenment and are the framework for the entire Buddhist doctrine. They are called "truths" not because they should be taken as self-evident facts, but because anyone can experience and realize them for her/himself. This teaching deals with suffering and how to overcome it, a process that is often compared with the healing of a physical illness. The first noble truth, the *truth of suffering*, is the illness itself; the second, the *cause of suffering*, is the cause of the illness; the third, the *end of suffering*, is the prescription; and the fourth, the *eightfold path*, is the medicine. The first two truths are the problem, the next two truths the solution. The Buddha said that we need to acknowledge our suffering and anguish, to understand how it arises, to learn how to rid ourselves of its causes, and to cultivate a path to awakening. This is the challenge of Buddhism.

THE FIRST NOBLE TRUTH—The Truth of Suffering

All life involves suffering. There is the suffering of birth, the suffering of sickness of old age and death, the suffering of the transient nature of things, and the pervasive suffering of existence itself. All beings, not just humans, share these kinds of suffering. There are three main types of suffering:

1. **Manifest Suffering** This type of suffering is easy to recognize. It encompasses all our pains, illnesses, losses, and mental and emotional disharmony.

2. **The Suffering of Change** It is only through change that one can come to understand this kind of suffering. These experiences appear to have the quality of happiness, but as Geshe Tsultim Gyeltsen points out, "Such happiness is very short-lived, like the dewdrop on the tip of a blade of grass, because the moment the sun comes out, it is bound to disappear." Just as suffering changes into happiness, happiness also changes into suffering.

3. The Suffering of Conditioning This is a far more subtle kind of suffering. Tibetan Buddhists believe that we are each a product of our previously created actions in past rebirths. The conditioning here is not just the social conditioning wrought on us in this lifetime, but the conditioning of innumerable previous lives having to do with the very fact of having a physical existence. Lobsang Gyatso compares the experience of this kind of suffering to a fish who, having been free to swim in the ocean, finds itself caught in a net. "Being caught in the net acts as the basis for its suffering." Yet, however ingrained these sufferings may seem, they all stem from the mind. It is said that with the proper view and the right method, everyone has the power to eliminate them.

THE SECOND NOBLE TRUTH—The Cause of Suffering

The second Noble Truth seeks an answer to the question "Where does suffering come from?" The causes are said to be: (1) karmic actions contaminated by delusions (see Chapter 6), and (2) the delusions themselves, which include attachment/desire, anger, and our fundamental ignorance. In order to cease karmic actions that cause suffering, we must cease the afflictive emotions or delusions that cause them. Our delusions or afflictive emotions are largely the result of not comprehending the impermanent nature of all things. This understanding is not just a general intellectual agreement that nothing lasts, but a profoundly personal comprehension of the fleeting nature of everything around us. Our houses, our bodies, our family, our friends: All are borrowed and all will eventually be returned. As the sutras tell us:

Like a star, an optical illusion, or a flame,
A magic trick, a dewdrop, or a bubble,
Like a dream, a flash of lightning, or a cloud—
So should one consider all compounded things.

We are one of those bubbles that the sutras refer to; we may suddenly burst at any moment.

There is also a *subtle* impermanence that is not as easy to see as the kind we can understand from observing the changing world around us. Lobsang Gyatso writes that "when a light is twirled in a circle fast enough, the eye does not see the motion, but only the circle of light." In the same way, we generally see things as static and don't observe the changes going on at subtle levels. If we can rid ourselves of our habitual grasping at stability, our minds become more free. When we decrease our attachment to a static world, we align ourselves with the nature of things, which is to change. This is why the great Indian poet, Shantideva, advises us, "Fix this firmly in your understanding, all that may be wished for will fade naturally to nothing."

It is said that the cause of all our delusions is *ignorance*, the mind conceiving phenomena in a way that does not accord with reality. This is not just a reference to impermanence. Our minds do not understand the interdependent nature of all phenomena, including the "self" (see Chapters 8 and 9). Based on such misconceptions, the mind grasps at permanently and inherently existing realities. From this wrong view, negative emotions arise, which lead us to perform negative actions. An example would be someone becoming angry and attacking another person. Ignorance about the true nature of the situation causes the delusion (anger), which in turn causes the negative action (violence). This series of causes and effects also turns back on itself as the negative action of violence causes negative *karma*. This negative karma increases delusions and the cycle begins again.

THE THIRD NOBLE TRUTH—The Cessation of Suffering

The third truth states that if suffering is caused by ignorance, anger, and attachment, then it follows that to find an end to suffering, we must first find an end to the causes of these delusions. The third truth acknowledges that we can indeed be cured of our suffering, because our delusions are not inherent in our minds and can be removed. The third Noble Truth is the prescription against suffering, but a prescription by itself is not enough. In order to be cured we must actually take the medicine.

THE FOURTH NOBLE TRUTH—The Truth of the Path

The fourth Noble Truth offers the healing, the means by which liberation from delusions can be attained. The Noble Eightfold Path is a lesson plan in wisdom, ethics, and meditative skill. These three aspects encompass the entire Wheel of Dharma, with its central axis of ethical discipline, its stabilizing rim of meditative concentration, and its sharp spokes of discriminative awareness or wisdom.

1. **Right View**

   Understanding the interdependent and empty nature of phenomena, including the self;

2. **Right Intention**

   Developing the right attitude and motivation;

3. **Right Speech**

   Not lying, gossiping, or engaging in harsh or divisive speech;

4. **Right Action**

   Engaging in virtuous activity and not engaging in non-virtuous activity;

5. **Right Livelihood**

   Following a line of work that does not harm others and that leads to a development of the other aspects of the path;

6. Right Effort

Developing a level of perseverance that is maintained over time;

7. Right Mindfulness

Developing a continual awareness of one's own state and one's environment and the ability to overcome distractions in one's meditation practice;

8. Right Concentration

Achieving the concentration required to achieve mental stabilization in one's meditation practice.

The Wheel of Life

Like those who journey on the road,
Who halt and make a pause along the way,
Beings on the pathways of the world,
Halt and pause and take their birth.

—SHANTIDEVA

The wheel of life is the cycle that relentlessly spins all living beings through repetitive states of birth, death, and rebirth. This is *samsara,* the merry-go-round of existence. Samsara means "to circle." Its meaning can be interpreted on a number of different levels, from the literal to the allegorical, but for many Buddhists samsara is seen as a symbol of a process that occurs in the mind. In Tibetan iconography this process is depicted as a giant wheel. The goal of the Buddhist is to escape from this repetitive cycle, which is seen as a mundane and limiting state, and discover *Nirvana,* the state of ultimate freedom. To do this, a Buddhist practitioner must develop a clear understanding of the limitations of samsara, and strive to understand what Tsong Khapa meant when he wrote, "Cherish knowledge of the chains that bind you to the wheel of cyclic existence."

In paintings of the Wheel of Life, Yama, the Lord of Death, clutches the giant wheel between his claws and holds its topmost curve between his fangs. His presence is a reminder of the inevitability of death and the impermanence of all phenomena within his grasp. In the top left of the painting is a moon, symbolizing the peace and coolness of enlightenment beyond the heat of suffering. In the top right corner stands the Buddha pointing at the moon, symbolizing the path to Liberation. The wheel itself is made up of a large outer circle in which three concentric circles form four separate bands. At the hub of the wheel are three animals: usually a cockerel, a snake, and a pig. The cockerel is a symbol of desire, the snake represents anger, and the pig, who holds the other animals' tail ends in its mouth, symbolizes ignorance. This is the engine room of samsara, and the animals represent the *Three Poisons* or mental delusions that power the wheel and keep beings caught in cyclic existence. Under the sway of these influences, most beings fail to see the defects of their current condition. It is said that if they did, they would attempt to escape samsara as if from a burning building. Around the hub of the wheel is a smaller circle, the right half of which is dark, symbolizing nonvirtuous action.

This half depicts people being dragged down by ropes into the rounds of rebirth. The left half of the circle is white, symbolizing virtuous action and shows people being led off the wheel by enlightened teachers.

THE SIX REALMS

The central band of the wheel is the thickest and is divided into six sections like pieces of a pie: three on the top and three on the bottom. These are the *Six Realms* or dimensions of existence in which different classes of beings reside: hungry ghosts, hell beings, animals, humans, gods, and demigods. These beings are associated with the various mental sufferings of greed, anger, ignorance, desire, pride, and jealousy. The six realms can be compared with psychological states, and it is not difficult to recognize these forces at one time or another existing in ourselves and in those around us. These states are karmic visions, experiences of life that are determined by an individual's actions in this and other lives. Thus they are ultimately created by our own minds. The top three sections depict the three "happy transmigrations," the relatively fortunate realms of humans, demigods, and gods. The lower half show the three "unhappy transmigrations," where the hell beings, hungry ghosts, and animals are born.

1. Realm of Hell (Anger)

This is a realm of intense misery, in which beings are dominated by feelings of anger and hatred. These beings exist in a state of total paranoia and see the world around them as dangerous and threatening. They live in a world of violent torment and are said to suffer extremes of temperature, unbearable environments of scorching heat and freezing cold. These conditions represent the emotional experience of violent burning rage and pitiless cold-heartedness. There is no room for compassion in this realm, as the unbalanced mental state of the inhabitants continually throws them into emotional turmoil.

2. Realm of the Hungry Ghosts (Greed)

The hungry ghosts are pathetic creatures who exist in a world of eternal dissatisfaction. They are endlessly seeking to feed their insatiable hunger and quench their thirst but can never find any relief. They are depicted as beings with round, distended bellies and long thin necks who are completely obsessed with their own needs and frantically seek to fill the chasm in their lives. They experience a world of constant denial and lack, but cannot see that it is their own perception that keeps them in this torment. Although they are surrounded by nourishment, they perceive food and water as pus and blood and therefore will not touch it. In the same way, they are unable to recognize the true sustenance of the Buddhist teachings that could lead them out of their pitiful state.

3. Realm of the Animals (Ignorance)

The animal realm is a state in which beings are dominated by unconscious reflexes and a certain ignorance, which makes it easy for others to exploit them. This realm is governed by base physical impulses that center around food and sex, which make it difficult for any higher feelings to develop.

4. Human Realm (Desire)

The human realm is the lowest of the three higher realms. Here, beings are driven by all the delusions of the other realms, but especially by the delusion of desire. We humans are depicted as falling between the extremes of attraction and aversion, trying to get what we want and to avoid what we don't. Yet we are not as completely stuck in our obsessions as beings in other realms. All beings in all realms have the potential to transcend their suffering, but it is the human realm wherein lies the greatest possibility for Buddhahood as the conditions for practicing the Dharma are more favorable.

5. Realm of the Demigods (Jealousy)

The demigods are subject to envy, so this is a realm of inter-personal strife where everyone is competing with one another.

The demigods are constantly comparing their lot with that of those around them, and they always feel that they have less than they deserve.

6. Realm of the Gods (Pride)

The gods reside at the pinnacle of samsara. This realm is devoid of obvious signs of suffering and appears to contain only ceaseless beauty and sensual pleasure. Here everyone is healthy and good-looking and leads a comfortable life full of exotic pleasures. They are not gods as we know them in the Olympian sense, for although they do possess some supernatural abilities, they do not have the power to intervene in human destiny. In describing the inhabitants of the god realm, Lama Edward Kunga Vantassel writes, "There is something obviously trivial about them....Their ability to use their senses to discern the relative reality of the world is strangely impaired. Their downfall is their pride and their fall is inevitable." It is said that right before each god plummets into a lower state of rebirth, their garlands of flowers begin to die, their bodies begin to smell unpleasant, and the other gods abandon them to their fate.

The rim of a wheel is where most of the movement occurs, and on the Tibetan Wheel of Life it is where the life cycle of all phenomena is depicted. The rim is separated into twelve sections, each containing a scene that illustrates a part of the process by which every living being comes into existence and remains spinning in samsara. These are called the *Twelve Links of Dependent Origination*, because each one connects to another like the links of a chain. As it says in the sutras, "Because this exists, that arises; because this is produced, that is produced."

THE TWELVE LINKS OF DEPENDENT ORIGINATION

(1) The **Ignorance** of grasping at inherent existence (symbolized by a blind person), leads to (2) volition or **karmic actions** (symbolized by a potter), which leave a karmic imprint on the mind and conditions one's (3) **consciousness** (symbolized by a monkey). This consciousness then leads to the creation of psycho-physical constituents or aggregates, to (4) **name and form** (symbolized by two people in a boat), from which arises the (5) **sense fields** (symbolized by a large house) of eye, ear, nose, tongue, body, and mind. These then make (6) **contact** (symbolized by lovers embracing) with the objects of the senses; the eye with sight, the ear with sound, the nose with smell, and so on. Contact leads to (7) **sensation or feeling** (symbolized by a man with an arrow in his eye), which in turn leads to judgments about what is good and bad, pleasant and unpleasant. In this way, feeling creates (8) **attachment** (symbolized by a man drinking alcohol), which leads to the act of

(9) **grasping** (symbolized by someone picking fruit) at the object of desire. This grasping becomes the foundation for (10) **existence** (symbolized by a couple in a tent) and leads to (11) **birth** (symbolized by a couple making love). This stage begins at conception, which is also the first stage of (12) **aging and death** (symbolized by an old man). At death the mind is plunged into ignorance once again, and the cycle begins anew. There are other presentations of the twelve links that start the cycle from a different point. Like on a circle, there is no one place that is the beginning of the process.

In Tibetan, the word Nirvana means "state beyond sorrow," suggesting that it is a condition of ultimate peace, beyond the suffering of samsara. Yet, on another level, Nirvana and samsara are the same place seen from the enlightened and unenlightened points of view. Samsara is nothing other than the way things appear to us. When the true nature of reality is understood, one sees what the second century Indian master, Nagarjuna, meant when he wrote "There is nothing whatsoever differentiating samsara from Nirvana. There is nothing whatsoever differentiating Nirvana from samsara."

RENUNCIATION

If a prisoner is used to her/his cell, s/he may consider it quite comfortable and gradually even forget about finding freedom. The thought of escaping might never enter her/his mind. Likewise, if one never desires to escape from the prison of cyclic existence one will remain there. Therefore, the defects or drawbacks of samsara (such as the three types of suffering discussed in chapter 4) are used as a topic for contemplation to help develop renunciation, the desire for Liberation. The practitioner develops "a mind of definite emergence"—a feeling of joyful renunciation of the chains that bind her/him to cyclic existence. Renunciation in Tibetan means "authentic becoming." It does not necessarily mean living in isolation from the world. What one renounces are the delusions that keep one from becoming one's authentic self and from attaining Nirvana.

Tsong Khapa tells us that without the attitude of renunciation, one cannot fully experience compassion for other beings trapped in the sufferings of cyclic existence and so will be unable to develop a powerful wish to free them from this suffering. To experience renunciation one must abandon the "Eight Worldly Concerns" such as the desire for praise or success (see Chapter 11). The core instruction for overcoming these concerns is meditating on one's own impermanence and death. "You will have to leave it all behind and go on later," said Milarepa. "Why not make it meaningful and leave it all right now?"

Karma

The happiness we all want and the suffering we
*   all try to avoid*
are produced precisely by our own actions.

—**DALAI LAMA XIV**

Karma is the fuel of samsara. It means simply "action," and the law of karma is the universal principle of actions and reactions, or causes and effects. Karma is the thoughts, words, and deeds of our everyday lives. Everything we do is karma. The teachings of Buddhism suggest that we should not look for answers to our problems in something outside of ourselves, nor are we merely victims of circumstance in a random universe. Our day-to-day actions form the foundation upon which all change takes place, and these alone are the cause of our happiness and suffering. The symbolism of seed and fruit is often used to depict the karmic process. Our actions are likened to a seed that does not grow without the right conditions. In the same way, all actions (including the actions of thought and speech) will eventually bear karmic fruit when the proper circumstances arise. When we reap the effects of our actions, it is said that our karma has "ripened," and the fruit can be sweet or sour, depending upon our conduct.

Our karma is not only the set of actions we have performed in this lifetime but those performed throughout all our lifetimes. According to the Buddhist view, this life we are living now is just one of countless lives that we have lived before. We have killed, died, and given birth over and over again. "If you collected all the tears of sorrow and anguish you have shed in past lives," says the Sublime Dharma of Clear Recollection, "they would make an ocean larger than any in this universe." Every being in existence has, according to Buddhist tradition, been our mother in a former life—a concept which offers an inkling of the vast extent of the rounds of rebirth. Our behavior in this life will determine our lot in the next life. The Buddha said, "What you are is what you have been, what you will be is what you do now."

The law of karma doesn't simply operate on an individual level. There is also collective karma, the karma of institutions or countries, which determines shared experiences of suffering or joy. The karmic principle of cause and effect acts upon everything in the universe. It is not a system of reward and punishment that occurs somewhere outside of us, but is a self-organizing process, a natural law by which the balance of everything is maintained. There is no concept of a creator in Buddhism—a separate divine force that directs earthly existence—and there is nothing that can be self-created. Everything comes into being as a result of certain conditions. As long as one remains on the wheel of life, one will perform actions and thus create more karma. Not all actions are cause for rebirth, however, only actions contaminated by basic ignorance. Yet, we must begin by committing even contaminated positive actions that will help to purify our negative karma. We should not abandon all actions altogether, but determine which ones are useful in our spiritual development. There are four criteria that must be present for an action to be considered complete and thus create a full karmic effect: (1) there needs to be the predetermined intention to carry out that action; (2) there needs to be preparation for it; (3) action needs to be performed; and finally, (4) there needs to be a sense of satisfaction at having completed it. For example, for the act of stealing to be entirely negative, all four conditions must be present. There are also degrees of negative and positive actions. Someone might lie, for example, so as not to hurt another person's feelings, and thus less negative karma is not accumulated.

The law of cause and effect does not offer a predetermined and fatalistic view of life. On the contrary, the very meaning of the word karma—"action"—challenges us to be creative and offers a participatory and victimless approach to life. When we experience pain, pleasure, joy, or discontent, it is to ourselves that we should first look for an explanation. Once we take responsibility we can actively change our karma, and thus change our future experiences in this and in other lives. Tibetan Buddhists see human life as very precious, because it is the realm which affords us the best possibility for enlightenment. Human birth is described as a "rarely found great ship," and the chances of incarnating as a human being are said to be so minuscule as to make the event almost miraculous.

The theory of reincarnation was well developed in Hinduism, but the tradition of recognizing a continual line of reincarnated teachers such as the Dalai Lama is unique to Tibet. Certain extraordinary individuals are believed to be able to consciously choose the time, place, and nature of their rebirth instead of simply being helplessly thrown into one. In the thirteenth century, the Karmapas of the Kagyu school began giving explicit information about where, when, and to whom they would be reborn. In Tibet, such high lamas are called *Tulkus,* those who choose to continue to reincarnate into a particular lineage. Prospective candidates for such titles are subjected to rigorous testing to discover whether they are indeed the true incarnation.

It is believed that the Buddha developed himself spiritually through numerous lifetimes before he became Shakyamuni Buddha. There is a story about one of his former lives in which he was also a young prince. One day, while walking in a forest, he stumbled upon a starving tigress who was so weak that she was unable to feed her cubs. The Buddha felt such enormous compassion for her plight that he lay by her side and offered himself to her as food. When it was clear that the tigress didn't even have the strength to tear his flesh, he cut his own wrists and fed her with his blood. When she was revived, he then offered his entire body to her. It is said that the tigress and her cubs were reborn as Shakyamuni Buddha's first five disciples.

When we understand the law of karma we see that it lies at the root of all our experience. We recognize what Kalu Rinpoche describes as, "the unfailing connection between what we do now and what we experience later." In understanding that our experiences are determined by our actions, we learn to refrain from engaging in negative actions and to attempt to perform more and more positive ones. The Dalai Lama says that we should not underestimate the value of even the most seemingly insignificant positive actions.

PURIFICATION

Negative action has one good quality—
it can be purified.

—TIBETAN SAYING

Even though we commit a negative action, we can stop it from ripening into a negative karmic reaction by purifying it. The

Tibetan folk hero Milarepa was a mass-murderer, yet he was able to purify his negative karma and become enlightened in a single lifetime. The Sutras say, "There can be no fault so serious that it cannot be purified by the *four powers*." These powers are also known as the four opponent forces.

1. **The Power of Regret** This comes from understanding the harm that the negative action has caused. This is not guilt, which suggests a negative and impotent state of mind, but "intelligent regret," which is a positive and creative mental state aimed at correcting the impure action.

2. **The Power of Support** This refers to those towards whom our negative action was directed; either Buddha, Dharma and Sangha or other sentient beings. Thus, to correct the negativity, one takes Refuge (see Chapter 7) and generates Bodhicitta (see Chapter 10).

3. **The Power of the Antidote** The antidotes are the positive actions of body, speech, and mind such as meditations that one engages in to purify the negativity.

4. **The Power of Resolve** This is the ongoing determination never to repeat the negative action in situations that formerly provoked it.

Taking Refuge

Taking refuge is the gateway to the Dharma.
—DILGO KHYENTSE RINPOCHE

Taking Refuge is a practice that is found in all schools of Buddhism. In the Tibetan tradition, it is what distinguishes a seeker from a true Buddhist practitioner. Taking Refuge is the act of aligning oneself with the path by placing a reasoned trust in the principles of Buddhism. A practitioner can take Refuge in a formal way, before her/his teacher, but s/he is encouraged to repeat the Refuge prayer often, especially as a preparation to meditation. Before a practitioner takes Refuge s/he should have already explored the value of Buddhist practice and philosophy and have developed a deep regard for its power and efficacy in relieving suffering. Edward Kunga Vantassel describes taking Refuge as "the refinement of an impulse that is at the foundation of our being," for the purpose of this practice is to orient the mind toward its ultimate goal—complete Enlightenment.

Buddhist practitioners take Refuge in the Three Jewels: the *Buddha,* the *dharma*, and the *Sangha*. Each object of refuge has a number of levels of meaning but, generally speaking, the Buddha is the teacher, the Dharma is the path, and the Sangha are companions on the path. By taking Refuge one is not investing in some external authority. As Pema Chödrön writes, "Taking Refuge does mean finding consolation in [the Three Jewels] as a child might find consolation in Mommy and Daddy. Rather it's a basic expression of your aspiration to leap out of the nest." The Dalai Lama states, "What is of prime importance at the beginning is to develop a deep conviction in the Three Jewels in general, and in particular, the possibility of achieving Dharma, Buddha, and Sangha *within ourselves.*" (italics mine)

THE BUDDHA

The jewel of the Buddha is not only the historical person, but represents all Buddhas—"protectors of beings"—throughout time and space. The Buddha is considered a worthy refuge because he conquered all obstacles to spiritual development, including belief in a separate self, negative emotions, and even death. He represents the perfected self who has mastered the path to enlightenment and is now able to reveal this path to those who sincerely seek to travel it. In taking Refuge in the Buddha, one is taking refuge in all of his qualities, and is attempting to cross the bridge between the Buddha and one's own Buddha-nature.

THE DHARMA

The Dharma is the means to Enlightenment, both the teaching and the practice. The *Dharma of Transmission* is the Buddha's teachings as revealed in the Tripitaka. The *Dharma of Realization* is the understanding of those teachings through contemplation and meditation. The Dharma is available for everyone without exception, for it "illuminates all beings impartially, like the light of the sun and moon." Taking Refuge in the Dharma is aligning one's deepest aspirations with the path of Buddhist practice once one has determined that this practice is effective. Just as when one is climbing a ladder, one doesn't always have to look up to make sure that the next rung is there, so a Buddhist practitioner develops a faith based on experience and reason that the ladder of Dharma will take her/him where s/he wants to go.

THE SANGHA

The Sangha is the instrument of the Dharma. Its collective and individual purpose is the passing on of the music of enlightenment from mind to mind through time and space. As a source of Refuge the Sangha is the spiritual community of holy

beings, such as Bodhisattvas and anyone who has directly realized emptiness. As a general term it refers to ordained Buddhist
practitioners. These are our spiritual allies who guide us along
the path to Enlightenment and redirect us when we wander
from the true way.

FAITH

Faith does not take the central role in Buddhism that it does in
some other religions, but that is not to say that faith is unnec-
essary. There is no room, however, for blind faith, only faith
based upon reason and individual investigation. Faith is viewed
as a technique rather than a goal in itself. It is a kind of mental
clarity and is included as one of the virtues of a Buddhist practitioner. Faith is described as a mind free from laziness, worry,
desire, negative thoughts, and doubt. Initially, the practitioner
forms a reasoned faith in the power of the Three Jewels from
observing the positive results of her/his practice. Eventually,
one transcends the need for belief when one gains direct experience of things formerly only assumed. As Nagarjuna said,
"Through faith one relies on the practices. Through wisdom
one truly knows."

The quality of one's own understanding will determine the
level at which a practitioner is able to approach the Refuge
practice. Reasons for taking Refuge include, in order of spiritual evolution, fear, faith, and compassion. A practitioner with

limited understanding will take Refuge out of fear, a practitioner with moderate understanding will take Refuge solely from faith, while a practitioner of advanced understanding will take Refuge largely out of compassion.

Faith acts as a kind of magnifying glass through which every positive quality can be enhanced. It can be used as a tool to bypass the ego, which always seeks rational explanations. However, for a Mahayana practitioner, faith goes hand in hand with intellectual reasoning. Thus it is useless to recite the refuge formula without first reflecting on its meaning. There are four stages in the development of faith: (1) *Clear Faith*, (2) *Aspiring Faith*, (3) *Confident Faith*, and (4) *Irreversible Faith*. *Clear Faith* is when you first feel inspired and excited about the spiritual potential of the Three Jewels. *Aspiring Faith* is when you aspire to actually use the Three Jewels to liberate yourself and others. *Confident Faith* is when you truly discover through personal experience the power of the Buddha, Dharma, and Sangha to free yourself and others from suffering. Finally, *Irreversible Faith* is when this faith remains unshakable under any circumstance no matter how difficult, including death.

THE PRACTICE

The visualizations adopted for this practice vary depending upon the preferences of the practitioner. For some, it is more beneficial to engage in complex visualizations of many beings such as Buddhas, Bodhisattvas, and lineage masters. For others, it may be better to visualize a single figure, such as the Buddha Shakyamuni, in which all the qualities are combined. Sometimes the spiritual mentor is added as a source of Refuge and is visualized as an emanation of the Three Jewels, a practice called the *Jewel Embodiment.* Whatever beings inhabit the field of our visualization, they should be imagined as gazing at us with kindness and encouragement. As one recites the formula, one imagines that one does so with all the beings in all the realms of existence. The basic refuge formula follows:

Sanskirt:	Translation:
Namo Buddhaya	*I go for refuge in the Buddha*
Namo Dharmaya	*I go for refuge in the Dharma*
Namo Sanghaya	*I go for refuge in the Sangha*

Bodhicitta, the altruistic mind, (see Chapter 10) is generated with the following Refuge prayer. When you recite this prayer, again imagine that you are surrounded by all sentient beings in existence and that you are reciting the refuge formula with them. Then visualize the Buddha entering the crown of your head and dissolving into you. The Dalai Lama elaborates on this practice: "Your body, speech, and mind become inseparable from those of the Buddha. Then you dissolve into emptiness; at that point meditate on emptiness and from within it arise into Buddha Shakyamuni, sitting on a throne." You then imagine that you have achieved spiritual union with the Buddha's qualities.

Another visualization one may adopt is to imagine the Three Jewels of the Buddha, Dharma, and Sangha in the form of rays of light that enter the top of the head and dissolve into oneself. As this happens, you experience yourself dissolving into emptiness and then coalescing into the form of an Enlightened being, a Buddha. Then, in a Buddha's form, you concentrate on generating infinite rays of light that transform all the surrounding beings into Buddhas also. This prayer is usually recited three or more times.

I go for refuge until I am enlightened
To the Buddha, the Dharma, and the highest Assembly.
From the positive merit that I collect
By practicing generosity and other perfections,
May I attain Buddhahood
To be able to benefit all beings.

The Wisdom of Emptiness

All things are realized when Emptiness is realized.
Nothing is realized when Emptiness is not realized.

—NAGARJUNA

"Emptiness" or "Selflessness" is the most popular translation of the Sanskrit word *shunyata,* but other translations include "suchness" and "space." The concept of emptiness is found in all schools of Buddhism, and its understanding is considered crucial to spiritual development. In the West, emptiness implies a lack of something, but this is not the case among Buddhists. As Alan Watts wrote, "Emptiness is not a void to be filled, but a window to be looked through." Buddhists do not regard emptiness as a philosophy or a point of view, but as the very condition of all phenomena. Emptiness or selflessness is nothing less than the way in which everything actually exists—the nature of reality itself that points to the interrelatedness and interdependence of everything in the universe. The line of reasoning goes as follows: There is nothing in the world that can exist independently of other phenomena. Everything that exists does so dependently. Therefore, everything is empty of independent existence. All is self-*less*.

In the *Heart Sutra,* the Buddha says that emptiness is beyond words or expression or thought. What this means is that emptiness cannot be talked about directly, but only in relation to something else. Emptiness and phenomena are inseparable, and to discuss emptiness at all one must use examples from the world of phenomena. When we watch a wave, for example, we can see that it is not independent from the ocean and that it really has no true separate existence. In the same way, other phenomena, no matter how distinctly they seem to exist, do so only in the same way as the wave—that is, in relation to a complex interplay of causes and conditions. Therefore, Buddhism teaches that nothing exists *inherently*.

To begin to develop a conceptual understanding of emptiness, we must first develop the suspicion that the manner in which we perceive the world is not necessarily the way the world really is. When we see an object such as a car, we at first perceive it as distinctly separate from the world, but when we examine it more closely, we find that this separateness begins to fade. We realize that we need to take into account the leather seats that were once the skins of live animals, the rubber tires that were living plants, the metal that came from inside the Earth we are walking on, the factory where it was made, the machine that fashioned it, the people who earn a living from its production. In fact, when we subject it to analysis, we realize that the number of influences that have come together to create what we call a car are practically infinite. We cannot really exclude it from the environment from which it was formed. Once we fully realize this, we still "see" the car, but its meaning for us has changed, and it seems less solid. According to this view, there is not even a single atom in the universe that has an independent existence. Every object and every event is part of the picture and exists relative to everything else. In fact, the theory of relativity has much in common with shunyata.

Once we are used to seeing objects in this way, we can begin to see the emptiness in our subjective states. We take this understanding from things outside us to things inside us— from mountains and raindrops to our fears and anger; from oceans and stars to our personalities; from weather systems to our loves and our hates. This doesn't mean that we don't have emotions, but we recognize their relative nature. Western Buddhists sometimes interpret these teachings as a call to seriousness, a negation of personality, whereas most Tibetan Buddhist teachers express emotion fully and spontaneously but not seriously, for they have learned the most profound lesson of all—the emptiness of the self.

We can begin to become aware of the subtle interrelationship between our consciousness and what we call reality by taking a look at how our mental labels create our experience. Where does one thing end and another begin? If you take apart a car piece by piece, at what point can you no longer call it a car? Where does music end and your experience of it begin? Where does your happiness end and another's begin? Our perceptual consciousness also plays an important role in isolating things from their environment by providing us with a visual outline. This outline becomes a basis for separation: the outline of cat becomes a cat, the outline of a table becomes a table. Apart from our visual perception, our emotional perception also contributes to the view of things as separately existing entities. The emotional value we place on things further emphasizes their independent reality for us. All these factors combine to form our ordinary view of the universe. We do not literally create the phenomenal world with our minds, but we do create an experience of separately existing objects and events that then becomes our reality. Buddhist teachings propose, however, that this conception of reality is merely a habit built up from lifetimes of conditioning and deep-rooted delusions. If we can learn to change our view, then there is an entirely different experience to be had—one which is in accord with a far more profound reality.

Emptiness in a Buddhist context is often misinterpreted to mean that nothing really exists and therefore nothing matters, and that our actions have no consequences, but Buddhist texts warn against such thinking. There is a difference between nothingness and no-*thing*-ness. Things certainly do exist, but they do not exist in the way we generally perceive them; that is, they do not possess an independent existence separate from everything else. In this way, our actions are far from meaningless. Their meaning is actually compounded, for their consequences reach farther than we ever imagined. At the other extreme is the idea that there is some ultimately existing divine reality and that the soul is an eternal entity. Buddhist texts describe these two interpretations, usually referred to as nihilism and eternalism, as the most commonly held wrong views of reality. Nihilism, or the negative extreme, negates too much, whereas eternalism, or the positive extreme, negates to little. Geshe Rabten explains that the first view "clings to annihilation," and the second "clings to permanence."

An intellectual understanding of the true meaning of emptiness is only the beginning, however, for to incorporate and fully realize the profundity of this view of reality is at least a lifetime's work. The implications of the philosophy of emptiness are truly enormous and can utterly transform how we view ourselves and those around us. We first become aware of the myriad influences that affect our actions and how we are the direct product of these influences. When we extend this insight to other people, we begin to develop a greater understanding and tolerance of their situations as we learn that they too are under the sway of a vast network of forces that we can barely begin to comprehend. The Dalai Lama has said, "When we consider that everything we experience results from a complex interplay of causes and conditions, we find that there is no single thing to desire or resent, and it is more difficult for the afflictions of attachment or anger to arise."

The level of realization when emptiness is experienced directly is translated from Tibetan as "complete joy." There is a complete letting go of all psychological, intellectual, and spiritual security—an experience that, when it is properly prepared for, brings with it a great freedom of mind. This is such a powerful realization that it can even break the chains of samsara; as Geshe Gyeltsen writes, "The wisdom of emptiness can sever the very root of cyclic existence." To develop a profound and lasting understanding of emptiness is not an easy task, and normally requires a practitioner to engage in advanced meditation practices. The Indian master Dharmakirti tells us, "The view of emptiness liberates, and the remaining meditations are means to achieve it." We must be wary, however, because of our psychological habit of solidifying things, not to regard emptiness as being *itself* somehow ultimately existent. As emptiness is the quality shared by all phenomena, it is also the nature of that quality. Hence, the texts speak of the "emptiness of emptiness." The subject of emptiness appears complicated because we are so used to our present mode of conception. However, it is said that even to develop a slight doubt that the way things appear to us is the way they actually are is very beneficial.

Wisdom in Tibetan Buddhism has a number of different meanings, but the most profound kind is the wisdom that realizes the truth of emptiness. Wisdom or *prajna* is usually represented by female deities and is symbolized by a bell. The bell is used in meditation rituals in conjunction with its male counterpart, an object called a *vajra,* symbolizing the method of compassion. There are three levels of wisdom:

1. **The Wisdom One Attains from Hearing**—Reception
   The more times one listens to a particular teaching the greater will be one's understanding on that subject. Many lamas say that when students attend a teaching on a familiar topic, even though they may not hear anything new, they will understand something new.

2. **The Wisdom One Attains from Thinking**—Contemplation
   This is the state of mind one achieves from reflecting deeply on the teachings.

3. **The Wisdom One Attains from Meditating**—Experience
   The only way to experience a clear understanding of emptiness is through meditation. It is the "unmistaken mind," the consciousness that understands emptiness as the true nature of reality.

These three levels of understanding are akin to the differences between hearing about space travel, thinking and studying about space travel, and actually having the experience of going into space.

THE TWO TRUTHS

The *Two Truths* are *conventional truth* and *ultimate truth*, or, put another way, *conventional* and *ultimate* realities. Conventional truth is the way that things seem—the appearance of things; absolute truth is the way things really are—their final mode of existence. These two truths do not contradict one another but, in fact, complement one another. Geshe Rabten uses the analogy of two planks of wood that are propped up against one another to form a triangle with the ground. These planks support one another and neither can stand alone. If one falls, so does the other. The ability of the planks to stand is conventional reality; their dependence upon each other is the ultimate reality.

Geshe Gyeltsen speaks about how, in ancient India, magicians created optical illusions to entertain people. They could conjure up beautiful creations of horses and elephants using only pebbles and twigs. The spectators whose visual perception had been influenced by the magician's incantations would *actually see* horses and elephants and believe them to be real. Similarly, ordinary beings only see conventional reality. For them, phenomena appear to exist independently and inherently and they also grasp at things as if they existed in that way.

The magician also sees the horses and elephants, but the difference is that he knows the tricks he is playing. Those who have gained insight into emptiness are likened to the magician, for they see both conventional and ultimate realities. Things appear to them as inherently existent but they know that things don't actually exist in that mode. Then there are people and beings who have realized emptiness directly and non-conceptually. In their meditative states on emptiness they perceive only ultimate reality. Things neither appear to them as existing inherently nor do they grasp at such existence. They are likened to the people who neither perceive nor grasp at the horses or elephants as being real because they aren't even at the magic show. Eventually, through meditation and training, the aspiring Boddhisattva learns to see through the lens of the middle view that transcends both inherent existence and non-existence. Duality is transcended and the two truths are united.

The Emptiness of the Self

*What we think of as "I" is a succession of
instants in a continuum of consciousness.*

—DALAI LAMA XIV

Selflessness in a Buddhist context is simply another word for
emptiness. Phenomena are described as being self-*less*; that is,
having no inherent existence. If emptiness, or selflessness is the
nature of all phenomena, then it follows that our own self-identity must also have this nature. However, because the idea of a
self is so central to our thinking, and because Tibetan Buddhists
regard the understanding of the emptiness of the self as central
to all Buddhist practice, the concept requires further explanation. In Buddhism, the causes of all suffering begin in the mind,
and by far the main cause of suffering is the false conception of
an independent and separate entity that we call the "I" or "self."

Belief in a separate self is described in Buddhist texts as the most basic form of ignorance and the strongest rope that ties one to suffering. It is the cause of all our anger, ignorance, and desire. The teachings compare our normal self-cherishing nature with a chronic illness, for which the only cure is the wisdom of emptiness. When we do not understand the spiritual beauty of emptiness, the idea that our self may be less real than we supposed can seem like a threat to our entire existence. As Sogyal Rinpoche writes, "In the depths of our being we know that the self does not inherently exist. From this secret, unnerving knowledge spring all our fundamental insecurities and fears." Yet Buddhist doctrine does not claim that we do not exist at all, only that we do not exist in the way we think we do. Our identification with a self is merely a habit, a way which we have been conditioned to experience life. One of the most profound insights in Buddhism is that there is another way.

The reason that we experience this self-referential point of existence is the combined impact of the *Five Aggregates,* the various aspects of the mind-body experience. They are our physical experience or form, plus sensation, perception, mental activities, and consciousness. It is considered important to understand the aggregates for meditation purposes so that one can learn to loosen attachments to mental states and emotional experiences.

THE FIVE AGGREGATES

1. **Form** This is the physical world of the elements (earth, water, fire, and air) plus the five senses (sight, hearing, smell, touch, taste) together with the experience of those senses. Thus this category includes forms which can be interacted with both physically and mentally.

2. **Feeling** This covers both physical and mental sensations or feelings that are classed as painful, pleasurable, or neutral.

3. **Perception/Discrimination** Once we experience these feelings and sensations we then discriminate between characteristics such as color, shape, or gender, and make judgments based on those differences.

4. **Conditioning Factors** These describe all mental activities including thoughts, memory, and other mental states.

5. **Consciousness** Consciousness is our awareness of all these things. It is classified into six types: eye consciousness, nose consciousness, ear consciousness, tongue consciousness, body consciousness, and mental consciousness. The senses themselves are not aware of what they are sensing; it is consciousness that holds an event and knows it as something that is seen or heard. The concept of one's own self-identity—the feeling of an "I"—is considered simply another aspect

of consciousness. There is also the basic consciousness that underlies all experience.

ANALYTICAL MEDITATION ON THE "SELF"

It is of no benefit merely to think that there is no separate independent self; one must apply one's own reasoning so that one's
conclusion can be firm. We are not denying conventional existence—otherwise we couldn't engage in this exercise! We are
denying the existence of an inherently and independently existing self. To do this we must conduct a thorough investigation.

Initially, we need to calm our mind using concentration
meditation. Then we apply analytical meditation (see Chapter
17). The process goes as follows. First we need to identify this
self whose nature we are investigating. We can do this quite
easily by thinking about something that we find upsetting or
something that we find extremely pleasurable. When we think
deeply about such things we will notice that strong feelings
arise and, with these feelings, a strong sense of identity. We
have found the self of our analysis. We allow ourselves simply
to observe this self-identity without judging it. We examine
how it appears to us and how we would describe it. Then we
turn our attention to the aggregates. We decide that the self
must be either the same as or separate from the aggregates.

Is the Self the Same as the Aggregates?

If the self is the same as the aggregates, then just as there are multiple aggregates, we would simultaneously experience corresponding multiple selves. The same problem would arise if the self were any one of the aggregates, for each has multiple aspects. When we investigate each aggregate, we cannot find the self in any one of them. For example, if the self is the body, then it would not be conscious. If it is the mind, then it is nothing but a jumble of mental activities that have no enduring qualities but are changing from second to second. If the self were the combination of mind and body, then we are postulating an even more complex combination of influences that have no united focus. The self becomes a collection and ceases to be a unitary entity. Yet, we experience a distinct and quite singular self that regards the aggregates as if they were its property. Also, the aggregates are always in a state of flux, but our self-identity seems to be more permanent. The self or "I" seems to be related to a consciousness, but it seems somehow more real than that consciousness and independent of it. When one concludes that the self is not the same as the aggregates, one begins to speculate whether in fact the self is separate from them.

Is the Self Separate from the Aggregates?

If the self is separate from the aggregates, then there should be no problem finding it. The self should be quite apparent, and

we should be able to point to it just as if a person we were looking for were to stand out from a crowd. However, we begin to
find that, as a result of our former analysis, the self, which at
first was so real, has become rather elusive. If the self is different from the aggregates, then it follows that it must be different
from our body, our feelings, our thoughts, our emotions, or our
awareness—in fact, from all of our experiences of life. If we
say that the self is something separate from all these things,
then we could never be aware of it, as all modes of awareness
are covered by the aggregates. If the self is separate from the
aggregates then it may as well not exist at all!

We realize that we cannot find a self that is separate from
or the same as the aggregates. There is no distinct and separate
master of our physical and mental experience. Our idea of the
self, of an "I" is simply that, an idea—a symbol of our existence that we have taken literally. We come to see that the self
is merely a label that we have attached to the physical and mental aggregates; it does not possess an inherent or separate existence. When we search for what is behind the label we see only
the result of our own misconception. When we have followed
this meditative analysis thoroughly and sincerely, we are simply left with the absence of an inherent self. This is not just a
vacuum; it is a totally new way of perceiving our habitual self-
grasping. This is the ultimate nature of the self and we should
allow our minds to become absorbed in this absence.

The concept of a separate, inherently existing self withers under such scrutiny. We begin to question what we formerly took to be self-evident. This realization is reinforced through meditation until it becomes part of a direct experience that doesn't have to go through intellectual or conceptual channels. Not only do we not need this false idea of a self; in fact it holds us back and limits our experience, causing us to identify with negative mental states. The Dalai Lama writes that the wisdom that understands selflessness "eliminates negative emotions simply through seeing phenomena as they really are." The concept of an inherently existing separate self is a filter through which we look at the world, and removing it is like entering another dimension. The teachings suggest that not only can we function quite happily without this false idea of a self, we can function in a way that fulfills our highest potential as human beings. The idea of a permanent self implies that one cannot fundamentally change. Without this idea there are far more possibilities. Also, if we dispose of the idea of a fixed self that exists separately from everything else, then we can realize greater opportunities for connecting with others and the world around us.

Through meditation, the idea of selflessness becomes gradually more familiar until it becomes a direct moment-to-moment experience. One can then apply this understanding of selflessness to the world. All phenomena—self and other—are understood to be essentially selfless or empty of independent or inherent existence, and all conventional perceptions of reality are replaced with this understanding. The Dalai Lama has said that all Buddhist thought and practice is contained within two principles: developing a view of the world that understands the interdependent nature of all phenomena, and leading a nonviolent life based on this understanding.

Compassion

All the joy the world contains
Comes through wishing happiness for others;
All the misery the world contains
Comes through wanting pleasure for oneself.

—SHANTIDEVA

Compassion, in Tibetan Buddhism, is an art, the masterpiece of which is a state of spontaneous, equinanimous love and understanding toward all beings, both human and nonhuman. However, Mahayana Buddhists also regard compassion scientifically, as the natural expression of a higher spiritual logic, without which there could be no Enlightenment. The eighth century Indian scholar, Kamalasila, wrote, "Compassion alone is the root cause of all the qualities of the Buddha," and the development of *great compassion,* the concern for the welfare of others over oneself, is viewed as essential to enter the Mahayana path. The Dalai Lama has said that there are no absolutes in Mahayana, but if there were one, it would be compassion.

Compassion is passion for all. It is not pity, which implies a fear of one's own suffering and an arrogance of being in some way superior. Neither is it a state of general indifference. Having no bad feelings toward anyone is not compassion. Compassion is an active state; a combination of love and the desire to help. The Dalai Lama has said that universal love is the desire for others to be happy, but that compassion is the wish that others be freed from suffering. When we see someone suffering greatly, we often experience a spontaneous burst of empathy and a desire to be able to do something about it. The Mahayana practitioner nurtures this feeling and develops it as a source of spiritual nourishment. S/he puts aside her/his needs for the needs of others and as a result is better able to overcome difficulties, while those obsessed with their own welfare find difficulty in dealing with the slightest problems. The experience of compassion engenders an understanding of the interconnectedness of all life. When we exercise compassion, we see not the separateness but the similarities between ourselves and all living beings. In the same way that we view our hands and feet as parts of our own bodies, those who have developed great compassion see other beings as parts of a living body. Thus the understanding of emptiness—the interdependence of all phenomena—arises from compassion. Compassion also arises from the understanding of emptiness, for once we see through the illusion of conventional reality, we experience compassion for those who don't. Tibetan Buddhism recognizes the validity of both approaches.

Only when one's compassion is spontaneous can it be called "great compassion." Having generated such compassion, the Mahayana practitioner then makes it her/his personal goal to develop spiritually in order to help others overcome their suffering. Shantideva writes that "concern for others is the way of the gods," and describes those who simply look out for themselves as "childish beings." However, this does not make the Mahayana practitioner proud or self-admiring. Compassion, when fully understood, is a humbling experience that involves dissolution of the ego, not reinforcement of it. Sogyal Rinpoche describes compassion as being the greatest ally in the war against self-cherishing.

This great compassion is described as the "unusual attitude," as it is rarely found. On examination, however, it is clear that while it is a potent force, compassion alone cannot relieve the sufferings of all living beings. Only a Buddha possesses this kind of power, and so the Mahayana practitioner aspires to become enlightened in order to fulfill her/his wish to end the anguish of all. This is the attitude of Bodhicitta.

BODHICITTA

Bodhicitta (pronounced *bo-dee-chee-tah*) means "heart of the enlightened mind," and it describes the quality of one's mind when one is focused on the goal of enlightenment for the benefit of other beings. The Dalai Lama describes Bodhicitta as "kindness combined with the highest intelligence." Once we have learned to generate this state of mind, the purpose of our lives is transformed. We begin to see obstacles and obstructions as opportunities to practice loving kindness, and in this way we use negative forces to enhance our spiritual practice. The Dalai Lama says that with a mind like this, "When we meet others, we do not feel claustrophobic and distant. On the contrary, we feel close to people....We are never afraid, but strong and courageous." As Shantideva writes:

Those whose minds are practiced in this way,
Whose happiness it is to soothe the pain of others,
Will venture in the hell of unremitting agony
As swans sweep down upon a lotus lake.

One practice for developing Bodhicitta involves reflecting upon the idea that all living beings have, in a previous incarnation, been the closest objects of our affection: our loving mothers or dearest friends. We see that these "mother sentient beings" are enduring great suffering, and we experience compassion for them and a desire to release them from their torment.

The Dalai Lama suggests that instead of turning away and protecting ourselves from suffering, we look at it directly. We can visualize any situation that we find unbearable, such as an animal being slaughtered, and develop the strong desire to free that being from its anguish. We don't dwell in this state but use it to extend our compassion to all beings, who, if not suffering this moment, are sure to experience suffering in the future. Finally, we actually commit ourselves to the task of working for their happiness. In this way we develop a sense of kinship with all life, a vast equanimity not contaminated by attachment.

Another practice is to contemplate how all living beings, no matter how seemingly insignificant, are equal, in that every being wishes for happiness and an end to suffering. Dilgo Khyentse Rinpoche writes, "With this compassion constantly in mind, we should perform every positive act...with the wish that it may benefit all living creatures without exception." These attitudes are not reserved for this world alone. The Dalai Lama says that the compassion of a Mahayana practitioner should extend "to the limits of the cosmos" and to "all beings throughout space." This attitude of mind, or Bodhicitta, is what determines if one is a practitioner of Mahayana.

ASPIRING AND ENGAGING BODHICITTA

There are two kinds of Bodhicitta: *aspiring Bodhicitta* and *engaging Bodhicitta*. Aspiring Bodhicitta is the wish to become enlightened in order to end the suffering of all sentient beings. Engaging Bodhicitta is achieved when one puts this compassionate wish for Enlightenment into effect by taking responsibility for this task and engaging in deeds which will lead one to Buddhahood. It is in this state that we recognize the Buddha-nature that lies within ourselves and every being. Shantideva compares these two types of Bodhicitta to two types of travelers: the traveler who is planning to make a journey is compared to the state of aspiring Bodhicitta. Engaging Bodhicitta is compared to someone who is actually traveling the path. The teachings describe aspiring and engaging Bodhicitta as being like the two wings of a bird, both of which are needed for it to fly. To generate aspiring Bodhicitta, the practitioner takes the following pledge:

From this time forth until reaching the site of awakening,
In order to ferry over the stranded, to release the bound,
To revive the breathless, to bring to nirvana those not
  yet in nirvana,
I generate a thought towards supreme, right and full
  great awakening.

THE BODHICITTA VOW

Generally, the practitioner first takes the Bodhicitta vow in the presence of the teacher. Later, s/he can take the vow in front of symbols of the Buddhas at an altar. It is regarded as efficacious to have a witness who accepts the individual's pledge. With the taking of this vow, the practitioner attempts to generate engaging Bodhicitta, the radiantly compassionate mind.

Teachers, Buddhas, Bodhisattvas, listen!
Just as you, who in the past have gone to bliss,
Conceived the awakened attitude of mind,
Likewise, for the benefit of beings
I will generate this self-same attitude.

It is not sufficient to generate Bodhicitta now and then for it to be called the awakening mind; it must become part of the very fabric of one's being. Only when one's compassion is spontaneous and effortless can it be called "great compassion." The practitioner who makes the sincere and enduring pledge to relieve the suffering of others has developed Bodhicitta and has entered the first of the *Five Paths* to Buddhahood.

Practices for Developing Compassion

When both myself and others
Are similar in that we wish to be happy
What is so special about me?
Why do I strive for my happiness alone?

—SHANTIDEVA

Practices for developing compassion are plentiful in Tibetan Buddhism. No practitioner will be able to experience engaging bodhicitta right away, but s/he can develop it through training and familiarity. "Our Bodhicitta may not yet be spontaneous," writes the Dalai Lama. "It is still something we have to fabricate. Nevertheless, once we have embraced and begun to develop this extraordinary attitude, whatever positive actions we do…while not appearing any different, will bring greatly increased results." Even when we have taken the Bodhicitta vow to assume responsibility for releasing every being from suffering, we need to understand that at present we do not have the power nor the ability to undertake such a task. Although we may have the desire to work to benefit other sentient beings, we need to be realistic about where we are on the path. In order to help others, we need more than the desire to do so. In fact, says the Dalai Lama, "altruistic thoughts can become an obsession and increase our anxiety." What we need is a method.

In Tibetan Buddhism, compassion can emerge spontaneously, but it is usually borne from an understanding of the interdependent and impermanent nature of reality. There are a number of practices aimed at inspiring feelings of compassion. Geshe Gyeltsen advises that we check in with ourselves three times a day: in the morning, around noon, and again before we go to bed. We should ask ourselves, Have my actions been positive or negative, kind or unkind? Gradually we learn to extend our compassionate actions from humans to animals to the smallest insects, for even the tiniest flea is with us on the path to awakening. A practitioner can also make offerings of fresh flowers or water bowls at an altar every morning while making the wish to attain enlightenment for the good of all other beings. *The Eight Verses on Thought Training,* by the Kadampa master, Langri Thangpa, present contemplations and meditations on compassion as follows:

VERSE 1:
Seeing Others as the Foundation for Our Practice

By thinking of all sentient beings
As even better than the wish-granting gem
For accomplishing the highest aim
May I always consider them precious.

In the first verse, we reflect upon the fact that our achievement of enlightenment completely depends upon the presence of other sentient beings. Geshe Gyeltsen explains that "Without sentient beings, there is no compassion; without compassion there is no Bodhicitta; and without Bodhicitta, there is no great awakening." Shantideva says that sentient beings are equal even to the Buddha in the way they help us achieve the awakening of Enlightenment.

VERSE 2:
Seeing the Needs of Others as Supreme

Wherever I go, with whomever I go
May I see myself as less than all others,
And from the depth of my heart
May I consider them supremely precious.

This is an exercise to remove arrogance and pride. The danger of arrogance, writes Geshe Gyeltsen, is that it causes us to underestimate others. This is a great error, because Buddhas and Bodhisattvas may often appear disguised as ordinary beings such as children, animals, and even as inanimate objects such as bridges or works of art, in order to help beings in this world. In the commentary on the *Illumination of the Path to Liberation,* it says that we should consider everyone and everything like glowing embers hidden beneath the earth. However, we should not make the mistake of losing confidence and thinking of ourselves as less worthy than or inferior to others. Geshe Gyeltsen writes, "When we accept ourselves as the most humble being, extend our humility and accept oneself as the lowest, we gain strength; we do not lose strength." The text is simply trying to encourage us to put our own needs aside and begin to see the needs of those around us as of greater significance than our own.

VERSE 3:
Preventing Delusions

May I examine my mind in all actions
And as soon as a negative state occurs,
Since it endangers myself and others,
May I firmly face and avert it.

This verse refers to all actions of the body, speech, and mind. Whenever we do, say, or think something that generates negativity, we should immediately, without brooding on it, acknowledge our action and form the determination not to engage in such behavior again. In this way, the habits of negative action, speech, and thought are weakened, and we become used to performing positive actions.

VERSE 4:
Holding Difficult People as Dear

When I see beings of a negative disposition
Or those oppressed by negativity or pain,
May I, as if finding a treasure,
Consider them precious, for they are rarely met.

It is relatively easy to generate compassion for friends and loved ones and even for those toward whom we have neutral feelings, but it is extremely difficult to have compassion for those whom we dislike or who have mistreated us in some way. We tend to avoid difficult people, feeling that somehow their negativity will rub off on ourselves. This verse offers an alternative response, and that is to view difficult people as the heart and soul of spiritual practice, for they challenge us to develop our positive qualities. Says Shantideva, "Your enemy is the true provider of all your virtue."

VERSE 5:
Accepting Defeat

Whenever others, due to their jealousy,
Revile and treat me in unjust ways,

May I accept this defeat myself,
And offer the victory to others.

This verse suggests that we do not need to defend ourselves from attack by those who are jealous of us. Their jealousy is a sign of their own internal difficulties. It says nothing about us, but speaks volumes about the other person, who, because of their lack of self-esteem, should therefore be an object of our compassion.

VERSE 6:
Regarding Those Who Harm Us as Teachers

When someone whom I have helped
Or in whom I have placed great hope
Harms me with great injustice,
May I see that one as a sacred friend.

This is a difficult verse to comprehend. How can we view someone who harms us as a "sacred friend"? The reason for this in the Mahayana view, is that in providing us with an emotionally difficult situation, that person has helped to ripen our karma, which, if not actualized in this way, could develop into some far greater manner of misfortune. Such a situation challenges us to remain compassionate even in the most formidable circumstances.

VERSE 7:
Exchange of Self with Others

In short, may I offer both directly and indirectly
All joy and benefit to all beings, my mothers,
And may I myself secretly take on
All of their hurt and suffering.

This verse refers to the meditation practice of *Tonglen,* which means "giving and receiving." This is the heart method of all the compassion-generating practices and is described in the following section.

VERSE 8:
Seeing All Things as Illusion

May they not be defiled by the concepts
Of the eight worldly concerns
And aware that all things are illusory
May they, ungrasping, be free from bondage.

The Eight Worldly Concerns, described by Geshe Gyeltsen, are: (1) becoming elated when we are praised, (2) becoming unhappy when we are insulted, (3) becoming happy if we receive any gifts, (4) becoming unhappy if we don't, (5) becoming happy upon achieving fame or success, (6) becoming unhappy when we are unsuccessful, (7) becoming happy when we are comfortable, and (8) becoming unhappy when we are uncomfortable. The text is exhorting us to stop viewing our circumstances in terms of positives and negatives, so that we are free from the "bondage" of opposites. Once we have achieved this freedom through an understanding of the true nature of reality, we can be even more effective in helping others.

TONGLEN: Giving and Receiving

Doing Tonglen sweeps away the dust that
*   has been*
covering over your treasure that's always
*   been there.*

—PEMA CHÖDRÖN

Tonglen is a meditation practice in which the practitioner, attempting to generate Bodhicitta, actively chooses to take on the sufferings of others. One visualizes taking all pain, difficulties, and sorrows from sentient beings upon oneself and giving comfort, understanding, and happiness. The text instructs us to "secretly take on" these sufferings. In other words, a practitioner doesn't go around announcing that s/he is engaging in this practice, for this only encourages pride in oneself and suspicion and confusion in others.

First we need to contemplate the topics mentioned in Chapter 10, such as reflecting on the equality of ourselves and others. We can begin with our partners, our closest friends, and our family members. Once we have developed the practice to the point where we care as much for these people as we do for ourselves, then we expand the circle of our compassion to include those toward whom we have neutral feelings (acquaintances and strangers), and finally to those whom we actively dislike. We should then reflect upon the disadvantages of caring only for ourselves, understanding that our self-cherishing egoism is the cause of all suffering and unhappiness in our lives. We then contemplate the benefits of caring for and cherishing others. We see that this attitude is the source of all happiness and the key to the door of Enlightenment.

During these contemplations, we learn to change our point of reference. Instead of seeing ourselves as passively receiving happiness from the world, we begin to see ourselves as actively transmitting happiness toward it. We get used to giving what we normally keep to ourselves. We begin to take more and more responsibility for our own experiences, both good and bad, and so begin to free ourselves from the idea that we are somehow a victim of fortune. Pema Chödrön says that in Tonglen, "You are cultivating a fearless heart, a heart that doesn't close down in any circumstance."

Some people might feel nervous about engaging in Tonglen practice, thinking that meditating upon the suffering of others will increase their own pain. It is true that being reminded of another's suffering can be a painful experience, but this does not mean that we are going to be somehow magically afflicted by the suffering we are visualizing. If we engage in this practice for someone who is suffering from cancer, for instance, this doesn't mean that we will get cancer ourselves! We should also bear in mind that whatever we experience is the result of our own actions, our karma. Doing this practice creates spiritual merit, and therefore can only improve our karmic future.

We should not avoid doing this practice because we think that we are the one who is suffering. Palden Gyatso, a monk who was tortured in Chinese prisons in Tibet for thirty-three years, said that it was the practice of Tonglen that helped him to survive. The Dalai Lama has said that he has carried out this practice for many years and has found it to be not only perfectly safe but extremely beneficial for his spiritual development. All we need to do Tonglen, says Pema Chödrön, is to have experienced one second of happiness and one second of suffering. However, if we experience resistance to this practice, it simply means that we are not quite ready for it. We can begin with the first stage of the practice and gradually build to encompass the whole meditation. Or we can practice taking on our own suffering and then expand the meditation to others. The following is an abbreviated version of this practice.

TONGLEN MEDITATION

Whoever wishes to quickly afford protection
To both himself and others
Should practice that holy secret:
The exchanging of self for others.

—SHANTIDEVA

Visualizing the Six States of Existence

The beings in the six realms can be seen as metaphors for our own mental negativities, and the kinds of sufferings they experience as representing the afflictions that we experience under their influence. We imagine the anger and hatred experienced by the beings of hell, the greed and eternal dissatisfaction of the hungry ghosts, and the ignorance and slavery of the animal realm. We visualize the human sufferings of desire and attachment along with all the problems of the human condition, the jealousy and feuding of the demigods, and the confusion and anguish of the proud gods when they fall from grace and plummet into the lower realms.

Actual Meditation

In the Tonglen meditation we attempt to enlarge the arena of our compassion. We begin with our closest friends and family members, and then we extend our compassion to include everyone we know. Then we extend it even further to include the whole population of the country, the Earth, the solar system, and to the beings in all realms of existence. We develop this universal imagery in our minds to create the universal heart. Geshe Gyeltsen says that we should especially focus on the physically and mentally ill, the homeless, and other social outcasts.

Receiving

We visualize that the sufferings and negativities of all these beings take the form of black smoke. This smoke travels from these beings toward us, merging to form a black cloud. In the center of our heart we visualize our own suffering and mental afflictions in the form of a black spot. Through our nose we breathe in the black cloud of the suffering of others. We then visualize this cloud and the spot inside our heart dissolving into one another and canceling each other out. We should feel a powerful sense of having been purified and of having helped others to achieve a state of peace.

Giving

As we exhale out through the nose, we visualize healing white light rays emanating from our heart toward the suffering beings. These rays represent the essence of all our love, health, and happiness. The moment these rays come into contact with the beings, they are completely transformed, and each being receives a healing according to its own need.

By engaging in this practice, one begins to see oneself as less and less important, and as a result one's own sufferings decrease in significance. Yet, practitioners must guard against feelings of pride caused by feeding the ego with the self-image of a savior of the universe. For this reason it is better to begin with people one knows and expand gradually. We shouldn't have too many expectations about the outcome of this practice or become disillusioned if, for example, the situation of a person for whom we are doing the practice doesn't improve. The point of Tonglen is to learn to cherish others and to transcend self-centeredness. The immediate transformation is not in others, but in the individual who is doing the practice. Ultimately these other beings do receive a benefit, for Tonglen helps one to develop the compassion needed to become enlightened, and an enlightened person is in a position to help all beings. However, there may be other influences at work during such a practice, for studies have suggested that those for whom people pray heal more quickly than those who aren't the beneficiaries of others' prayers.

The Nature of Mind

The essential nature of your own mind is pure.
—DALAI LAMA XIV

The nature of mind is described in Buddhist texts as having both *conventional* and *ultimate* modes of existence, just like all other phenomena (see The Two Truths p.71). Sogyal Rinpoche describes the dual nature of mind using the image of a vase. The space around the vase is the mind's ultimate nature, and the space inside is the mind's conventional nature. When we shatter the walls of the vase through meditational practice, they merge into one "mindstream," an experience of supreme bliss. However, the walls of the vase are merely a symbol of our own misperception through which we have learned to see things dualistically—as being separated into subject and object and having inherent or independent existence.

In Mahamudra, an advanced meditation practice of the Kagyu and Gelug school, there is a level of realization called "one taste," which involves dissolving the perceived barrier between subject and object. The reason that we don't experience this dissolution on a daily basis, but remain in dualistic consciousness, is said to be due to the "four faults": (1) The mind is too close to be recognized; (2) The experience is too profound to comprehend; (3) The true nature of mind is too simple to believe; and (4) Enlightenment is too wonderful for us to accept.

The ultimate nature of mind is described in terms of the five elements of space, fire, earth, water, and wind. The element of space is the mind's emptiness or voidness. This voidness has unlimited potential, and this illuminating potential is connected to the element of fire. All experience is rooted in the mind, just as plants are rooted in the soil, and so the function of mind as the foundation of all experience is connected to the element of earth. The mind is also dynamic and changeable, and this quality is associated with the element of wind. Water is associated with the mind's adaptability and continuity, like a river that conforms to the shape of the rocks and ground and flows on ceaselessly.

There are said to be two main obstacles to Buddhahood: the *obscuration of delusions*, emotions that keep the individual tied to the wheel of birth and death, and the *obscuration of omniscience*, the ignorance that blocks one from knowing the true nature of reality. The latter are described as extremely subtle influences in our psyche that cause us to perceive things in a dualistic way. All these afflictions and obscurations, however, are regarded as temporary or adventitious, for they do not have the power to penetrate into the essential nature of the mind, which is beyond all dualism. Just as the dirt on clothes can be washed away, so can the mental defilements be cleansed from our minds. The dirt and the clothes are not the same thing; likewise our mental defilements and afflictions are not the same as our minds. If they were, then there would be no possibility for Enlightenment. Through developing our innate wisdom, we learn to discriminate between our egos and our ultimate nature. Said Kalu Rinpoche, "As a mother gives birth to a child, so the mind, once its nature is discovered, gives birth to Enlightenment."

Every person and indeed every sentient creature is said to carry within them the *tathagatagarbha*, the seed or embryo of Enlightenment. This seed of Enlightenment is the potential to become a Buddha. The teachings speak of a mythical bird, the *garuda*, who enters the egg already completely formed. This bird symbolizes our Buddha-nature, which although already full grown and perfect, cannot fly until it hatches from the egg of ignorance.

THE THREE BODIES OF A BUDDHA

A being who has become enlightened has the ability to function on many levels of consciousness. A Buddha can operate simultaneously in three planes of existence: the universal, the ideal, and the individual. These are known as (1) the *Dharmakaya* or *Truth Body,* (2) the *Sambhogakaya* or *Enjoyment Body,* and (3) the *Nirmanakaya, Emanation* or *Form Body.* (The Sambhogakaya and Nirmanakaya are sometimes collectively referred to as the *Rupakaya, or Enlightened Form Bodies.*)

Dharmakaya—The Truth Body

The Truth Body of a Buddha is related to the quality of mind's emptiness. It is the combination of all the Buddhas' positive mental qualities, the ultimate aspect of mind that arises from perfect wisdom. The Truth Body is the field of ultimate reality experienced in profound states of meditation. "Your own mind, aware and void inseparably, is Dharmakaya," wrote Patrul Rinpoche. All Buddhas share this body of absolute reality. It is the universal reality of what Lama Anagarika Govinda calls "primordial law." The Truth Body is the nondual mind of a buddha free from all obscurations and empty of inherent existence. It is the ultimate aspect of the Dharma, and it is from the Truth Body that the Enjoyment Body and Form Body are manifested.

Sambhogakaya—Enjoyment Body

When the Truth Body is experienced, then the ideal character of a buddha is realized. This is the Enjoyment Body of a Buddha, sometimes called the *Rapture* or *Bliss Body*, and it is related to the mind's quality of clarity. This perfect body resides in a field of nonmaterial existence called a *Pure Land* or *Buddha field,* a realm that benefits from a Buddha's direct influence. A Pure Land is the ideal world of pure compassion and ultimate wisdom that a Buddha has created through numberless acts of wisdom and compassion. When a being has realized the Enjoyment Body or enjoyment field, s/he sees everything as being an aspect of her/his own mind. The enjoyment body is the Buddha that Buddhists aim to contact in their meditations: a being who has transcended birth and death, and who exists in a realm that can be accessed through a loving heart and a disciplined mind.

This world of ours is also a Pure Land, for even the most impure realm exists in potential perfection. It only appears imperfect because of the imperfect minds of its inhabitants. The Pure Land is immediately available to us, but we do not see it. When we purify our minds we realize that the Sambhogakaya is not a cosmic Eden, but the condition of an enlightened mind. From the combination of the Truth Body and the Enjoyment Body flows Nirmanakaya, the Form Body.

Nirmanakaya—The Form Body

The Form Body or Emanation Body of a Buddha is related to the quality of mind's unimpeded manifestation. Just as light is the spontaneous expression of the sun, so is the Nirmanakaya the spontaneous expression of Enlightenment in physical form. It is the material world of everyday life, and yet it is far from mundane. The Form Body or "Body of Transformation" appears in the world as enlightened teachers, including the historical Buddha, and also as material objects of the Buddhas' compassion, such as medicine, food, works of art, or even whole planets. The Nirmanakaya is the compassionate appearance of physical reality.

The Five Paths

Abandon evildoing; Practice virtue well;
Subdue your mind: This is the Buddha's
teaching.

—THE SUTRAS

The Five Paths outline the stages of spiritual progress followed by both Hinayana and Mahayana practitioners, and
encompass a large part of the Buddhist Dharma. Dharma is a
word that has multiple meanings, some of which are
"change," "transformation," and "support." It can refer to the
realization of the enlightened state and also to the path that
leads there; however, the term is generally used to mean the
teachings of Buddhism. Geshe Rabten says that when someone saves another person's life or gives food to a hungry
stranger, whether they believe in religion or not, they are

practicing Dharma. Ultimately, says Lama Norhla, "All Dharma is taught as a remedy to ego-clinging."

View, *meditation*, and *action* are the "three pillars of the dharma." The first necessity for a Mahayana practitioner is to establish the proper approach to reality or "right view"—the first step on the Noble Eightfold Path. The Dharma is a vehicle for acquiring this view, which the practitioner attempts to assimilate into her/his own experience through meditation. The eventual result is the ability to maintain this view continually no matter what difficulties arise. Through meditative practice and contemplation, one learns to bridge the gap between the dharma and one's mind, until one is not simply receiving teachings but experiencing one's own truths. In this way, one's actions will reflect one's understanding. A Buddhist practitioner takes certain vows that relate to her/his level of commitment. There are the Hinayana vows of individual Liberation, the Bodhisattva vows of the Mahayanist, and the Tantric vows of Vajrayana. There are five basic commitments of a Buddhist lay person: (1) vow not to kill, (2) vow not to steal, (3) vow not to lie, (4) vow not to engage in sexual misconduct (that which causes harm to another), and (5) vow to avoid intoxicants, especially alcohol.

The Buddhist tradition lays a great emphasis on the importance of discipline. Discipline is a commitment to a way of life that chooses certain actions over others. Initially, this discipline may require effort, but eventually, it arises naturally from one's understanding. As this understanding grows, so does one's commitment, in the same way that as a tree grows, so do its branches. However, the teachings recognize that there may be rare circumstances when we have the moral obligation to break one of these vows "and in such circumstances," says the Dalai Lama, "we are not only permitted to transgress a vow but it is our duty to do so." The Mahayana path involves: (1) establishing a connection with the teachings, (2) taking Refuge in the *Three Jewels* (see Chapter 7), (3) developing Bodhicitta, and (4) developing meditation skills.

One travels Five Paths using the combination of the *skillful means* of compassionate transmission of knowledge and the intuitive *wisdom* to see through the illusion of separate existence. They are: (1) The Path of Accumulation, (2) The Path of Preparation, (3) The Path of Seeing, (4) The Path of Meditation, and (5) The Path of No More Learning.

THE FIVE PATHS

1. **The Path of Accumulation** Here the practitioner gathers what s/he needs for the journey to Enlightenment. On this path one accumulates merit from virtuous thoughts and actions and wisdom from hearing and contemplating on the teachings. If s/he has not already done so, the practitioner also cultivates the meditative

stability of *calm abiding*. This is the ability to meditate without becoming disturbed, to be able to concentrate one's mind on an internal focus of attention, and to engage in intricate visualizations (see Chapter 17).

2. **The Path of Preparation** When the object of the meditator's focus is the emptiness of inherent existence in all phenomena, and when this meditation leads to the experience of calm abiding, then one has entered the *Path of Preparation*, sometimes called the *Path of Application*. The meditator develops an ever-deepening understanding of emptiness during four stages: (1) warmth, (2) peak, (3) endurance, and (4) supreme realization. During the warmth stage, the meditator has a conceptual understanding of emptiness. In the peak stage, this conceptual understanding increases, and one's spiritual virtue becomes indestructible. In the endurance stage, the meditator faces and overcomes any fears that arise out of the understanding of emptiness as the ultimate truth. When the meditator reaches the stage of supreme realization, subject and object are realized as being aspects of the same reality and s/he enters the next path. Kalu Rinpoche says that while one is on the paths of Accumulation and Preparation, "there is a growing sense of freedom, just as if a person in prison were to have his or her bonds and manacles

removed and, though still imprisoned, were free to move about the cell."

3. **The Path of Seeing** Kalu Rinpoche describes the experience of the Path of Insight as resembling the opening of the prison door. Up until this point, the meditator has only experienced the *idea* of emptiness. On the *Path of Seeing* one experiences it directly. In between meditation sessions one still perceives duality, but one's understanding has become nondual. At this stage, one is said to have the ability to choose one's future rebirths. The meditator overcomes cultural conditioning but still harbors the traces of misperceptions from numerous lifetimes, which are far more deeply ingrained. It is from the Path of Insight that one enters the first of the ten levels or "grounds" of the Bodhisattva called the "Very Joyous."

4. **The Path of Meditation** At this level, the aspiring Bodhisattva develops the ability to enter into advanced meditative states. It is on this path that one achieves the remaining nine levels of the Bodhisattva.

5. **The Path of No More Learning** At this point one has attained the supreme condition of Enlightenment and become a Buddha, so there is no more learning to be done. A being at this level simultaneously manifests omniscient consciousness (Truth Body), a pure,

metamaterial form (Enjoyment Body), and a physical manifestation (Emanation Body). "It is impossible to describe the transcendent state of a Buddha with words," says Nagarjuna. "Ordinary beings cannot even begin to imagine it."

The Bodhisattva

*Once we have escaped samsara, we can return
out of compassion and love for sentient beings.
We can return as a bodhisattva.*

—Geshe Tsultim Gyeltsen

Bodhisattva is a Sanskrit term that means "one who aspires for
Enlightenment," but it was translated into Tibetan as "Enlightenment hero." Tibetans regard this figure as a cosmic spiritual
warrior. A Bodhisattva is not a mythic character, however, but
a living breathing entity who represents the innate potential in
all of us. Bodhisattvas are "children of the Buddha," who are
motivated by Bodhicitta, the wish to become Enlightened for
the sake of others. They are Buddhas in training who tirelessly
pursue the stages of the path, gradually developing their spiritual capacities until they become Enlightened.

The first step on this path is developing aspiring Bodhicitta and taking of the *Bodhisattva vow,* when a practitioner pledges to continue to be reborn until there is not a single unenlightened being remaining. Aware that this is an infinite task, the practitioner aims not only for personal nirvana, but the Nirvana of "great compassion" in order to help all beings end their suffering and become free from cyclic existence. This pledge reinforces and stabilizes one's Bodhicitta. Bodhisattvas aspire to attain the body of a Buddha, to be, as Robert Thurman puts it, "effortlessly capable of freeing all beings from suffering and of transforming the entire universe into a Buddhaverse of perfect opportunity for the happiness of all."

A Bodhisattva does not reject Buddhahood in order to remain in samsara and help other beings. What the Bodhisattva does reject is personal Liberation as an end in itself, and thus s/he attains a more complete form of Enlightenment. A Bodhisattva works upward for Enlightenment and works downward for others, yet s/he does not cling either to the world or to Enlightenment—to samsara or to Nirvana. In the *Essence of the Middle Way,* we read:

Because they see its defects, they avoid samsara.
Because their hearts are loving, Nirvana will not hold them.
The wise who wish the happiness of beings dwell even
in samsara.

A Bodhisattva is a wandering mendicant of the mind. As the teachings say, "In form, in feeling, will, perception, and awareness, nowhere in them they find a place to rest on."

The goal of the Bodhisattva is to free all beings from samsara, but to have the power to do this, one must first free oneself. The Dalai Lama suggests that an aspiring Bodhisattva begin by avoiding the *ten negative actions* and practicing the *ten positive actions* (see Chapter 15). The actual Bodhisattva path has three stages: (1) entrance, (2) training, and (3) accomplishment. The entrance is taking the Bodhisattva vow and developing Bodhicitta. Training involves the practice of the six *paramitas* or "perfections," which include disciplines of ethics, meditation skills, and the development of wisdom. A Bodhisattva in training also needs to develop "skill in means": the ability to adapt the method of teaching to the specific needs of the recipient. Accomplishment is the attainment of Buddhahood.

The Sakya scholar, Togmey Zangpo, wrote the *Thirty-Seven Practices of a Bodhisattva* six hundred years ago. Geshe Gyeltsen describes these as a Bodhisattva's "thirty-seven essential job descriptions." They involve advanced spiritual practices, such as accepting the negative karma of others. Geshe Gyeltsen explains, "If we are beaten nearly to death by somebody, without any wrongdoing on our part, the consequences for that other person will be disastrous when that karma matures. Understanding this, strong compassion arises, and we can accept that negative deed as part of our own negative karma."

THE BODHISATTVA VOW

The *Bodhisattvacaryavatara*, or *Guide to the Bodhisattva's Way of Life*, is one of the greatest religious poems ever composed. It was written by the eighth-century Indian master, Shantideva, and it incorporates the three main sections of the Buddha's teaching. In it he presents the extraordinary attitude of mind of a Bodhisattva. This attitude is one that Mahayana practitioners attempt to develop, in all circumstances and toward all beings.

May I be a guard for those who are protectorless,
A guide for those who journey on the road;
For those who wish to go across the water,
May I be a boat, a raft, a bridge.

May I be an isle for those who yearn for landfall,
And a lamp for those who long for light;
For those who need a resting place, a bed;
For all who need a servant, may I be a slave.

May I be the wishing jewel, the vase of plenty,
A word of power, and the supreme remedy.
May I be the trees of miracles,
And for every being, the abundant cow.

Like the great earth and the other elements,
Enduring as the sky itself endures,
For the boundless multitude of living beings,
May I be the ground and vessel of their life.

Thus, for every single thing that lives,
In number like the boundless reaches of the sky,
May I be their sustenance and nourishment
Until they pass beyond the bounds of suffering.

The Six Perfections

*It is vital to understand and develop
the deep conviction
that consciousness has the potential to
increase to a limitless level.*

—DALAI LAMA XIV

The Six Perfections, or paramitas, are part of the rigorous spiritual training program that a Bodhisattva embarks upon once s/he has generated bodhicitta, the mind of Enlightenment. The Six Perfections are: (1) generosity, (2) ethics, (3) patience, (4) effort, (5) concentration, and (6) wisdom. Sometimes, four more perfections are added: (7) skill in means, (8) aspiration, (9) power, and (10) superior wisdom.

1. The Perfection of Generosity

The suffering of guarding what we have,
The pain of losing it all.

—Shantideva

This practice concerns training oneself to release from attachment. It is the perfection of an attitude that does not hoard anything for oneself, and gives gladly and willingly without feelings of pride or regret. A Bodhisattva gives with confidence and respect, not only material things, but also her/his own spiritual merit—the positive karmic imprints gained from wholesome actions—for it is in sharing one's merit that one guards against losing it. Eventually, one learns to offer even one's own body in meditation without experiencing any resistance or attachment.

There is a story which illustrates how even the least generous person can progress in such a practice. One day, an extremely wealthy man came to see the Buddha. He was so miserly that he couldn't bring himself to give away even the smallest thing. The Buddha told the man to think of his right hand as himself and his left hand as another person and to pass small objects from one hand to another. Once the man was able to do this easily, the Buddha then instructed him to offer small presents to his own family. When the man could do this, he was then told to give things to his neighbors and friends. Eventually

he was able to give things away without hesitation and he
became renowned for his great generosity.

2. The Perfection of Ethics

Morality is like the earth.
It supports everything, animate and inanimate.
It is the foundation of all positive qualities.

—The Buddha

In Buddhism, morality is the desire not to engage in any harmful actions. The practice of the *Perfection of Ethics* involves
avoiding the ten negative actions and engaging in the ten virtuous actions. There are three nonvirtuous actions of the body:
(1) killing, (2) stealing, (3) sexual misconduct; four of speech:
(4) lying, (5) divisive speech, (6) harsh speech, (7) gossip; and
three of mind: (8) covetousness, (9) harmful intent, and (10)
holding distorted views. The ten virtuous actions are the opposite of these. Virtue and nonvirtue are defined not only by the
consequences of the action but by the motivation behind it.
Three conditions must be present for an action to be virtuous
or nonvirtuous. A negative act is considered nonvirtuous if,
(1) the person is motivated by negative thoughts and intentions,
(2) the person commits a negative action in a rational state of
mind, and (3) the person enjoys committing the negative
action. (A positive act is only virtuous if it is motivated by positive intentions). *Sila,* the Sanskrit word for *ethics,* means

"attainment of coolness." Training in ethics creates an inner peacefulness free from the heat of afflictive emotions. It prepares a foundation for meditative practice by stabilizing and disciplining the mind and helps the Bodhisattva to evolve spiritually on every level. As it says in the *Pratimoshka Sutra*, "just as a person without legs cannot run, a person without proper morality cannot gain freedom from cyclic existence."

3. The Perfection of Patience

There is nothing that does not grow easier through habit.
Putting up with little troubles will prepare me to endure
  much sorrow.

—Shantideva

The Bodhisattva learns that to be angry at the imperfections of others is, in the words of Shantideva, like resenting fire for its heat or resenting the sky for having clouds. S/he understands that the actions of other people are like forces of nature that arise from causes and conditions that are enormously complex. Also, one cannot develop patience without experiencing provocation. There is a story about the Tibetan master Patrul Rinpoche who visited a hermit. The hermit proudly told him that he had been meditating for twenty years on the perfection of patience. "That's a good one!" said Patrul Rinpoche. "A couple of old frauds like us could never manage anything like that!" At this the yogi became extremely agitated and demanded that the unwelcome visitor leave him in peace. "Where is your perfect patience now?" Patrul Rinpoche teasingly inquired.

"There can be no practice of patience without there being people who wrong us," writes the Dalai Lama. "How then, can we call such people obstacles to our practice of patience?... We can hardly call a beggar an obstacle to generosity." Yet, patience is more than being tolerant of others. As Geshe Gyeltsen explains, "If we go through immense hardship in the process of our practice, tolerating that hardship is also a form of patience."

4. The Perfection of Effort

If we don the unchangeable armor of enthusiastic
   perseverance,
Then knowledge will increase within us like a waxing moon.

—Tsong Khapa

Effort is necessary for any practice to be successful, but it is especially important for the beginner. Effort is the feeling of confident perseverance in the process. It generates endurance and, combined with patience, leads to positive changes. One must be careful not to expend all of one's energy at the beginning and then give up when there are no immediate results. What is needed is constant moderate effort. Initially, a practitioner may find that the necessary effort for practice is hard to muster, but eventually this will change and less and less effort will be required. The *Perfection of Effort* is achieved when one endeavors in one's spiritual practice without any sense of reluctance. Says the Dalai Lama, "It is finding joy in doing what is good."

5. The Perfection of Concentration

One must begin by searching for tranquillity,
Found by those who with joy, turn their backs upon the world.

—Shantideva

The concentration referred to here is the stability and clarity of the mind in meditative states. It is the ability to maintain an unwavering attention on the focus of the meditation (see Chapter 17).

6. The Perfection of Wisdom

The Bodhisattva's acts are boundless, as the teachings say.
The greatest of them all is this: to cleanse and purify
  the mind.

—Shantideva

A Bodhisattva requires the foundation of ethics and concentration to calm the mind and provide the stability for analytical reasoning into the nature of reality. The *Perfection of Wisdom* is the culmination of all the others. It refers to the analytic faculty of one who realizes the truth of emptiness, especially the emptiness of the self. The Bodhisattva uses her/his concentration to focus her/his attention on seeing through appearances and perceiving all phenomena as a combination of continually fluctuating aspects without a self-sufficient existence. When this wisdom is perfected to its highest degree, all ignorance is eliminated, and the Bodhisattva has become a Buddha.

The Ten Grounds of the Bodhisattva

There are ten levels, called the "ten grounds of the bodhisattva," which intersect the Six Perfections at various points and more intricately describe a Bodhisattva's progressive spiritual advancement. They are: (1) the Very Joyous, (2) the Stainless, (3) the Luminous, (4) the Radiant, (5) the Difficult to Overcome, (6) the Manifest, (7) the Gone Afar, (8) the Immovable, (9) the Good Intelligence, and (10) the Cloud of Dharma.

At the tenth level, one reaches Buddhahood (sometimes called the eleventh level). According to Dilgo Khyentse Rinpoche, Buddhas "are filled with spontaneous, non-conceptual compassion, and whatever they do, even a simple gesture of their hands, brings benefit....Working tirelessly for the benefit of all living creatures, they dredge the very depths of samsara."

Negative Emotions

If there is a cure when trouble comes,
What need is there for being sad?
And if no cure is to be found,
What use is there in sorrow?

—SHANTIDEVA

Negative emotions are viewed in Buddhist teachings as the direct result of our own faulty perceptions. If we understood the true nature of reality and were not trapped by the walls of our conventional belief system, then we would not have to suffer any emotional afflictions. We tend to look to external factors and blame others when we are upset, but since our minds cause the emotions, it is to our minds, not to external remedies, that we should look for relief.

The core reason for the experience of negative emotions is said to be our self-grasping ignorance, which causes us to see ourselves as separate and independent entities. There are a number of teachings and instructions aimed at putting afflictive emotions in a proper perspective. Experiences such as resentment can be seen as simply a nexus of influences that we have labeled, possessing no real substance. Holding on to negative emotions is considered illogical and ultimately destructive. "If you cling to a hurt," says Geshe Gyeltsen, "then you are hurting yourself again and again....Holding a grudge is another way of holding an illness inside us." Aryadeva, Nagarjuna's main disciple, says that someone under the influence of strong negative emotions is almost at the point of insanity.

A Mahayana practitioner learns to apply "antidotes" of philosophical reasoning and meditative concentration as soon as the thought connected to the negative emotion enters our head. We need to develop a more sensitive awareness, so that we can notice the first ripple of disturbance, however subtle. When a negative emotion or thought first develops, we are then able to apply the antidote right away. If we suffer from desire, for example, we learn to cultivate non-attachment by reflecting on the disadvantages of experiencing desire and by calming the mind in meditation. Negative emotions are a closing down of perspective. For example, when one is angry, the object of one's anger is seen as entirely negative, when a clearer analysis shows this to be untrue. Anger is regarded as ultimately self-destructive. Shantideva referred to his anger as, "My foe, whose sole intention is to bring me sorrow." Yet, practitioners learn to overcome anger by immediately applying the antidote of compassion. If anger arises in the mind, one can attempt to intervene before it gets out of control. Rather than maintaining our focus on the object of our anger, which only increases our negative state, we turn our attention to the anger itself.

Buddhist practitioners learn to see emotions in the same way as waves upon the ocean that rise and then subside back from whence they came. Rather than indulging our emotions or suppressing them, we simply observe them with acceptance and tolerance and allow them to return to the ocean of our mind. The same technique can be used for the object of one's anger. When we see someone else acting badly, instead of becoming upset with them, we can see that they are controlled by influences, which at present they are unable to comprehend. We understand that the person and the person's negative behavior are not the same thing. As Aryadeva wrote, "Buddhas see the delusion as the enemy, and not the childish who possess it." For Buddhists, negative emotions are the real enemy and to eliminate them is the truest victory of all. The Kadampa master Geshe Ben Kunkyen said:

I will hold the spear of mindfulness at the gate of the mind,
And when the emotions threaten, I, too, will threaten them;
When they relax their grip, only then will I relax mine.

There are an extraordinary variety of emotions recognized in the sutras (there are said to be twenty-one thousand emotional afflictions that arise from desire alone!), but there are five main negative emotions. These are the *Five Poisons*. They include the three found at the center of the Wheel of Life: (1) attachment/desire, (2) anger, and (3) ignorance, with two more of (4) pride and (5) jealousy. (Sometimes negative doubt is inserted instead of jealousy when the object of doubt is the truth of the dharma itself.) Attachment exaggerates the importance of an object, whereas pride exaggerates the importance of oneself—a situation that, if left unchecked, leads to jealousy. The desire to obtain Liberation should not be confused with ordinary forms of attachment, because the result Liberation offers is entirely superior. Wholesome emotions should not be confused with negative ones. We should foster our love and compassion and not make the mistake of thinking that these feelings are also delusional.

There are also twenty subsidiary emotional afflictions: (1) shamelessness, (2) rage, (3) greed, (4) concealment, (5) spite, (6) vengefulness, (7) cruelty, (8) inconsiderateness, (9) forgetfulness, (10) wildness, (11) distraction, (12) vanity, (13) carelessness, (14) lack of confidence, (15) hypocrisy, (16) laziness, (17) fogginess, (18) deceitfulness, (19) belligerence, and (20) lack of conscience. We should not become discouraged when negative emotions continue to arise. The practice of ridding oneself of negative emotions is long and arduous, and we should expect many difficulties, for we are taking on lifetimes of conditioning and habitual reactions. Yet, along the way, we can use our own experience of emotional suffering as a part of our practice. Unpleasant emotional experiences help to eliminate the negativities of the past, and from this perspective we can learn to accept them as a teaching. Turning suffering into an opportunity for understanding is called "transforming adverse circumstances into the path of Liberation." As Shantideva has said:

Suffering also has its value:
Through sorrow, pride is driven out
And pity felt for those who wander in samsara,
Evil is drawn back from, goodness seems delightful.

We first learn to recognize the seething morass of resentments, jealousies, and petty obsessions that occupy our minds. This discovery is like finding squabbling strangers living in our home, contributing nothing to the household and actually sapping our resources. The Buddha used a technique of philosophical reason to ward off these mental and emotional afflictions and to allow us to change the disharmonious nature of our internal home. This occurs through a process of realization and elimination. Once we realize the true nature of things, we are able to develop the confidence to work at eliminating the things that have kept us from this realization. As the Dalai Lama has said, once you don't have anxiety, you have energy.

Meditation

All suffering in this life and others
is created by the unsubdued mind.

—DALAI LAMA XIV

Meditation is a technique used to calm and develop the mind.
There are many different meditation methods to suit all kinds
of practitioners, but all methods are designed to break through
psychological conditioning and lead the practitioner from
ordinary perception to extraordinary perception. By training
the mind in this way, says the Dalai Lama, "we can transform the
way in which we act, speak, and think." Calming the mind
doesn't just mean having peaceful thoughts; it is a way of going
beyond ordinary thought altogether—to experience one's
innate natural clarity and radiance. When they first start to
meditate, some people might feel that they should be doing
something else with their time, something more "productive."

"Give time a rest," says Chogyam Trungpa. "Let it be wasted. Create virgin time, uncontaminated time." The reason being that, "There is no other way to attain basic sanity than the practice of meditation."

When a practitioner first begins to meditate, s/he may experience enormous mental upheaval and encounter even greater difficulties than before s/he started. This does not mean that the meditation is increasing one's difficulties, but that one is becoming conscious of them by developing a more subtle awareness. Geshe Rabten compares the beginning meditator to someone walking through a city street. From ground level it may not seem as if the street is very busy. But when one carries one's meditation practice further, one gains a greater perspective, as if viewing the same street from the roof of a building. From this vantage point one can observe things that one couldn't see from street level, and it looks as though there is much more going on. Yet, the street has not become busier. Only one's perspective has changed. Thoughts will inevitably arise during meditation, but the practitioner gradually learns to stop reacting to them. Sogyal Rinpoche advises the meditator to view thoughts with gentle tolerance, like an old man watching a child playing or an ocean looking at its own waves.

It is important to follow a method when practicing meditation. It is said that someone who tries to meditate without first gaining an understanding of what they are doing is like a man without arms trying to climb a rock face. The two main forms of meditation are *concentration meditation* and *analytical meditation*. In the beginning, the first will be the more difficult practice, as we are used to using our minds to analyze things, but we are not so used to focusing our attention on one thing for a long period of time. Concentration and analytical meditation are considered essential skills that the practitioner should master before moving on to more advanced meditative practices.

PREPARATION

During meditation sessions, the back should be as straight as possible so that the energy channels of the body are aligned. If possible the legs should be crossed, either in full or half-lotus position, symbolizing the unity of opposites. The muscles of the body should be relaxed, and the meditator should be able to sit without experiencing physical pain. One can use a chair if necessary. The hands should be at the level of the navel with both palms facing upward and the right hand resting on top of the left. The tips of the thumbs touch one another, forming a triangle; the nerve channel associated with Bodhicitta, the mind of Enlightenment, is said to pass through the thumbs. If the hands feel uncomfortable in this position, one can place a small cushion underneath to support them. Most meditations require the eyes to be open, although the gaze is lowered to an angle of about 45 degrees to keep the meditator from being distracted by surrounding objects. However, one may close the eyes if open-eyed meditation proves too difficult. The practitioner should not focus on anything in particular but should gaze out with an oceanlike expansiveness. The tongue rests lightly in the upper palate to ensure that one's mouth doesn't become dry during the session.

First, one should reflect upon the potential of Buddhahood not only in oneself but in all living beings. The meditator develops the deep conviction that the power to end all delusion and suffering exists within her/his own mind and s/he takes Refuge in the Three Jewels. To develop the proper motivation for meditation, the practitioner can recite the following prayer, called the *Four Immeasurables*:

May all beings have happiness and the causes of happiness,
May all beings be free from suffering and the
  causes of suffering,
May all beings abide forever in bliss,
And may all beings remain in equanimity without too much
  attachment or aversion,
Believing in the equality of all.

In Mahayana practice, it is also extremely important to "transfer merit." At the end of the session, one should dedicate whatever positive energy one may have accumulated during the meditation session to all other sentient beings. This acts as a continual reminder of the purpose of spiritual practice.

CONCENTRATION MEDITATION—
Calming the Mind

In concentration meditation the practitioner learns to stabilize the mind. "Most of the difficulties we face stem from a lack of mental control," says Geshe Rabten, and concentration meditation is a powerful method for taming the mind. One places one's mind on the focus of the meditation as if it were the only point of reference in the universe. The focus of the meditation, often called the "object" of the meditation, can be the ultimate nature of mind, the emptiness of the self, a focus of internal visualization such as a tantric deity or a white point of light, one's breath, or an external physical object such as a stone or piece of wood. If one can fix one's mind this way without distraction one has achieved the meditative stabilization of concentration meditation or calm abiding. It is called calm abiding because learning to concentrate to the exclusion of all else has a naturally calming effect upon the mind while the mind abides on the chosen object. Geshe Gyeltsen says that the serious practitioner can achieve a significant level of calm abiding in six months.

The two most commonly experienced hindrances to meditation are *laxity* and *excitement.* Laxity, also called "sinking," is a feeling of mental dullness, a fogginess which results in loss of internal clarity and which, if not corrected, will lead to sleep. Excitement is the opposite state, when the mind becomes overstimulated and scattered. Both are bad for concentration. The remedy for excitement is recollection or mindfulness–returning one's mind to the object of meditation as soon as the distraction occurs. The remedy for laxity is staying alert. These two—recollection and alertness—are essential for successful meditation, just as they are essential for success in one's everyday affairs.

NINE STAGES OF CONCENTRATION MEDITATION

These stages describe increasing levels of concentration that lead up to the realization of calm abiding. The nine stages are: (1) initial setting, (2) continual setting, (3) re-setting, (4) close setting, (5) invigoration, (6) pacification, (7) total pacification, (8) single-pointedness, and (9) formal setting.

In the first two stages, the meditator cannot focus her/his mind for more than a few moments without becoming distracted, and in the *continual setting* s/he can only do so for about a minute or so. At this point, excitement is the more common obstacle, but one may also experience laxity. The meditator uses the power of recollection or mindfulness to return her/his mind to the object. Within a single meditation session a practitioner may need to bring the mind back hundreds of times.

Gradually, one learns to concentrate for longer periods without becoming distracted by thoughts. In the stage of *re-setting,* one is able to "reset" her/his concentration using the power of recollection. The practitioner becomes increasingly aware of the distractions as they occur and becomes more skilled at overcoming them. However, s/he can still only concentrate for a few mintues at a time. During the fourth stage of *close setting,* no distractions are enough to completely break the meditator's concentration as the concentration is set "close in" to the object of its focus. One may still experience laxity, however, and must use the power of alertness to counteract it. Some meditators confuse the close setting stage with actual calm abiding, as it can lead to a very peaceful feeling.

Through the ensuing stages, the meditator increasingly is able to focus and concentrate. Mental energy and clarity increase, and the meditator experiences a greater peace of mind and inner contentment. By the seventh stage of *total pacification,* only the slightest effort is needed at the outset of the meditation session, after which the mind is so practiced that it spontaneously enters the meditative state. By the final stage of *formal setting,* the practitioner is able to meditate undisturbed for weeks at a time. S/he is nourished only by the "food of samadhi," and s/he experiences unprecedented ecstasy of body and mind. Says Geshe Rabten, "The mind becomes so clear that when we concentrate on any material object it is as though we can see each individual atom of it." However, even the bliss experienced in deep meditation can become an obstacle to further progress if we cling to it. We need to go beyond it to the profound insight of the ultimate nature of reality—emptiness.

Eventually, however, all concepts, even the concept of emptiness, must be let go of, so that this reality can become a direct and pure experience.

ANALYTICAL MEDITATION— Developing the Higher Insight of Emptiness

Once we have calmed and stabilized the mind, we can then investigate it, just as in order to study a frame of a film, we must first stop the reel. Those who think that meditation means maintaining a blank mind will not develop insight into emptiness. Many Westerners become interested in developing calm abiding meditation, but teachers say that only analytical meditation is capable of pulling up the roots of the ego. When we meditate on an object, we use analytical or *higher insight* meditation to dissolve the object of its conventional appearance and to see it as part of the entirety of existence.

The mind has now become a precision instrument that we can use to investigate emptiness—the ultimate nature of reality. The practice of analytical meditation leads to the development of various degrees of understanding of emptiness with which we can overcome all negative mental states. The meditator alternates concentration meditation with analytical meditation, and when the practice of analytical meditation actually *produces* calm abiding, the practitioner is said to have attained insight. If this insight occurs when the object of the meditation is emptiness, then the practitioner has entered the *Path of Preparation,* the second of the Five Paths to Buddhahood. The understanding of emptiness becomes less and less conceptual, until it is experienced directly, and the practitioner enters the Path of Seeing. The following exercises combine the methods of concentration and analytical meditation.

THE BREATH AS AN OBJECT OF MEDITATION

Six Stages of Breathing Meditation

These six stages are: (1) counting, (2) following, (3) placing, (4) investigating, (5) changing, and (6) completion. The following meditation is one recommended by Geshe Rabten.

    1. Counting We concentrate on our breathing. When we are able to count ten naturally paced inhalations without the mind wandering, we move on to the next stage.

    2. Following We mentally follow the breath, which is visualized as a thin line of smoke. We follow the inhalation with our mind as far as the neck and then follow the exhalation to a place just beyond the nostrils. After we can do this comfortably, we then follow the in-breath down to the chest and out an equal distance beyond our nostrils. We then follow the breath down to our knees and again, the same distance out of our nostrils. Then we mentally follow the breath down to our feet and out again the same distance.

3. **Placing** We are able to visualize the breath as a stationary line of smoke from the nostrils to the feet and we develop great control over our breathing.

4. **Investigating** We remain concentrated on the breath but part of our mind is able to investigate its nature, such as the particles and molecules that make up the air that we breathe in.

5. **Changing and 6. Completion** These stages are for very advanced meditators. At the completion stage one enters the Path of Seeing with a direct realization of emptiness as the ultimate nature of reality.

Watching the Breath

Sogyal Rinpoche offers another method for using the breath in meditation. In this practice we focus only on the out-breath. When we breathe out, we let the mind flow out gently and naturally with the breath. Between the out-breath and the in-breath we will begin to notice a natural gap before we breathe in. We rest in that space and continue resting there as we breathe in. We focus again on the out-breath and again we rest in the space during the in-breath. About 25 percent of our attention should be on the breath and 75 percent on relaxing into the space in between.

Geshe Rabten suggests another method apart from alertness for dealing with distracting thoughts during meditation: to simply observe the thought when it arises. "If we watch and observe the thought in this way," he writes, "it will eventually dissolve back into the nature of mind itself."

ANALYTICAL MEDITATIONS TO DEVELOP HIGHER INSIGHT

The Self as an Object of Meditation

During this meditation the practitioner concentrates analytically to investigate the nature of the self. One studies the five aggregates (psycho-physical constituents) one by one, determining whether or not they can encapsulate the idea of one's self-identity. Eventually, the meditator understands that the self is neither the same as nor different from these aggregates and as such does not possess inherent existence. One sees that the self is simply a label placed upon an intersection of continually fluctuating dynamics. With practice, this very absence of inherent existence of the self becomes the object of the meditation and the practitioner uses concentration meditation to rest in this nonconceptual state (see Chapter 9).

The Mind as an Object of Meditation

Here one works with analytical meditation and asks oneself, Where does mind come from? Where is it to be found? Is it inside or outside our bodies? How do thoughts arise? Where do they come from? When a thought disappears where does it go? Are the mind and its thoughts the same? The meditator avoids the temptation to judge the thought; s/he lets all thoughts arise, but s/he stops naming them. S/he is looking not at what they mean, but at what they are made of.

When the practitioner observes the mind during deep meditation, the mind seems to have the quality of formless space. Yet it has an additional quality of having the power of cognition, the ability to apprehend phenomena. "Observing the mind in this way is rather like looking at a clear piece of glass," writes Geshe Rabten. "We are able to see other objects through the glass but the glass is our main focal point....We are not merely concentrating on a blank mind or the absence of thought. There is an object, which is the clear and cognitive nature of the mind itself."

We can use the methods of recollection and alertness when we become distracted or lax in our concentration. When we lose our focus on the pure nature of mind, we can actually allow a thought to enter our head. This thought, like breath upon glass, enables us to recognize the mind once again and reaffirm our concentration. However, if the problem is excitement, and we become overwhelmed with thoughts, it may be better to look to their origin. "When you are completely barraged with thoughts," writes Dilgo Khyentse Rinpoche, "chasing after each one in turn with its antidote is an endless task." It is better, he says, "to look for the source of those thoughts, void awareness, on whose surface thoughts move like ripples on the surface of a lake, but whose depth is the unchanging state of utter simplicity."

REST PERIODS

When the mind becomes tired during the meditation, it is better to take a short break rather than to force oneself to continue. Fatigue leads to drowsiness and loss of mental clarity. If we don't stop our meditation before we succumb to this state, when we come to sit again, we will immediately remember the previous session's drowsiness and be uninspired to continue. The Dalai Lama compares the meditation session to a hearth. When the meditator takes a break s/he doesn't put the fire out completely, "so that when you rekindle the fire you will be able to do so quite easily and quickly." We can step outside for some fresh air, splash cold water on our face, and then return to the session. Gradually, as we develop in our practice, we will find that the experiences we have during our meditations begin to cross over into our everyday lives.

Tantra

By passion the world is bound,
by passion the world is released.

—Hevajra Tantra

Tantra is the dominant form of religious practice in Tibet. Tibetan Buddhism preserved the Indian Buddhist Tantric traditions, and each school has its own tantric practices. The Tantric vehicle can be called *Tantrayana*, *Mantrayana*, or *Vajrayana*. Tantra is the means applied to the wisdom of emptiness learned in the Bodhisattva training (otherwise known as the *Perfection Vehicle*), and its goal is the complete and utter transformation of the human condition.

Tantra means "unbroken stream" as it describes a continuum that takes a practitioner from ignorance to Enlightenment. Tantra is the collective term for a complex system of meditative practices that use the methods of ritual symbolic visualization for transforming one's experience of conventional reality. As the Buddhist scholar, John Powers, writes, "Tantric practitioners seek to overcome the pervasive sense of ordinariness that colors our perceptions of daily life." Tantra is described within a vast body of literature and so we will only touch upon the essential points here, the full meaning of which can only be appreciated by those who have penetrated its depths through practice and initiation. Of the three divisions of Buddhist doctrine—the Sutras (discourses), the Vinaya (discipline), and the Abidharma (metaphysical knowledge)—Tantra is generally considered to belong to the Sutras. It is in the Sutras that the Buddha taught meditative practices, and Tantra trains a practitioner in a special method of meditative stabilization. The Buddha is said to have given Tantric instruction while manifesting in the form of various meditational deities.

Tantra is regarded as the pinnacle of Buddhist teachings, and Tibetans consider its practices to be the most potent and efficient method for attaining Enlightenment. A practitioner on the classical Mahayana path is said to take an average of three "countless eons" to reach Enlightenment, whereas dedicated practitioners of Tantra can become Buddhas in only one lifetime. This is why Tantra is called "the gateway of the fortunate ones." Tibetan Buddhist teachers, including the Dalai Lama, say that participation in Tantric practices is vital to the path towards Buddhahood. However, Tantric practice takes an unusually strong mind and enormous compassion and is not for everybody. It is said that even Tantric practitioners with little ability have greater compassion and intelligence than the most able practitioners of the Perfection Vehicle.

Rather than avoiding pleasure in the things of this world, Tantra suggests that one partake of these pleasures as a way to turn enjoyment into realization. (Tantra is an extremely disciplined practice, however, and does not condone indulgent abandon.) Tantra regards every experience and every mental and bodily act, however mundane or even unsavory it may appear, as potential grist for the spiritual mill. "Vajrayana sees everything as sacred," wrote Kalu Rinpoche. "All appearance is a form of divinity, all sound is the sound of mantra, and all thought and awareness is the divine play of transcending awareness."

The Tantric practitioner thus uses emotions in order to transcend them. While most Mahayana texts speak of ridding oneself of desire through developing mental discipline, the Vajrayana path suggests that the practitioner actually use the feeling of desire as part of the spiritual path. Desire is regarded as an energy that can be redirected from nonspiritual interests to ones that can lead a person to spiritual emancipation. Just as a polio vaccination uses a quantity of the polio virus to build the body's defenses against the same disease, so Tantric practitioners use negative emotions as a tool to overcome them. However, just as in the field of medicine, Tantra requires great caution, for if one doesn't know how to transmute the energy of the emotions, one will end up with even more desire or anger than before!

The Tantric practitioner works with meditational deities who are considered emanations of the Enlightened mind. The meditator visualizes a Buddha, such as Avalokiteshvara, who represents the collective compassion of all the Buddhas, conjuring such detail so that it seems as if the deity were actually present in the room. The meditator begins by acknowledging the Buddha's extraordinary attributes: the Buddha's perfect speech, perfect body, and perfect mind, and the meditator may praise the Buddha and receive various blessings. Through a series of increasingly advanced meditation steps, the practitioner learns gradually to absorb the divine personality of the deity into her/his mind–a practice called "self-generation." The practitioner must remain aware, however, that the Buddha is not ultimately real but is empty of inherent existence. The practitioner's mind becomes one with the deity (an experience said to have the nature of extreme bliss) in an experience called "The Union of Appearance and Emptiness." The mind of the practitioner is transformed into the mind of a Buddha, and her/his environment is experienced as having been transformed into a *Pure Land*, in which everything is a manifestation of divine reality. As is says in the *Lamrim*, the texts that outline the path to full Buddhahood, "On every atom is found a

Buddha, sitting amidst countless Bodhisattvas," and the universe is an "infinite sphere of mystic beings."

The world is no longer perceived as a collection of separate objects. Subject and object are seen as a chimera, and subtle energies, which an advanced practitioner can manipulate to perform miracles, are perceived. The practice of Tantra is called *taking the result as the path* because the practitioner works with the resultant enlightened state while on the path to Buddhahood. The basic idea of Tantric meditation is that the more familiar one becomes with something, the more one can incorporate this into her/his life, until it eventually becomes second nature. Being surrounded with symbols that represent the highest aspects of ourselves is a continual reminder of these qualities.

Tantric practitioners should possess a solid foundation in the teachings of Sutra, especially the *Three Principle Aspects of the Path*—renunciation or the determination to transcend cyclic existence, Bodhicitta, and an understanding of emptiness. At least a conceptual understanding of the emptiness of self and phenomena is required before a practitioner can engage in Tantra. Without this, writes Robert Thurman, "One will be in danger of transferring the routinely frozen imagination from the ordinary objective world to a psychotic fixation on an extraordinary perfected world, and there will be no chance of becoming a successful Adept." There is a popular misconception in the West that the reason teachers warn against practicing tantra prematurely is that people might develop dangerous powers. It is far more likely that the unprepared person will send her/his weaknesses out of control.

THE IMPORTANCE OF A TEACHER

This is one of the reasons that it is considered essential that one learns Tantric practice under the supervision of a qualified instructor. No Buddha has ever gained Enlightenment without working with a spiritual mentor. In Tibet, this teacher is called a "Friend of Virtue." Tibetan Buddhists do not encourage faith without examination, and this pertains also to finding a spiritual mentor. We should examine the lama, and see if s/he has the qualities required. There needs to be much trust in the mentor-student relationship, and it is important for one to have confidence in one's teacher's abilities. Although it is possible that a practitioner can become enlightened by meditating on Buddhas, a working relationship with a lama is the key to fast and efficient progress. Unlike Bodhisattva vows, which can be taken by oneself, Tantric vows must be taken in the presence of a living person.

DEITY YOGA

In Tibetan Buddhism a meditational deity is called a *yidam*, which means "to link the mind." *Deity yoga* is the essence of

Tantra. To realize the enlightened state, a practitioner must do more than meditate on emptiness; s/he must meditate also on the Buddha's form. Deity yoga requires an active imagination, but it is not simply make-believe; it is a system of deep psychological training. A sense of *divine identity* must be cultivated whereby one regards oneself as an embodiment of the very deity one is visualizing. The Dalai Lama describes deity yoga as a rehearsal for Buddhahood that teaches a familiarity with the mind of Enlightenment. The qualities of a Buddha are perfected not step-by-step as in sutra practices but in combination—as divine totalities.

Tantra applies the theory developed in Sutra practices. It offers vital and immediate experience of everything that has been learned before. In Sutra, the methods of the Bodhisattva vehicle—practicing the Six Perfections and generating Bodhicitta and the wisdom of emptiness—complement one another but are not fully integrated. Deity yoga, however, involves a complete merging of method and wisdom, so that one learns to tap into the hidden resources of one's own mind. In Tantra, the method is deity yoga, and the wisdom is the mind that directly perceives emptiness. The union of method and wisdom is not seen as two separate aspects that have been combined but as a continuum in a single field of consciousness. Just as a magician isn't fooled by her/his own illusions, so the meditator understands that the meditational deities are essentially insubstantial. Like a magician, however, one still interacts with one's creations. Through meditation on the Buddha's form, one perceives the entire universe as a Buddha-field or Pure Land; through meditation on the Buddha's speech, one perceives all sound as the sound of mantra; and through meditation on the Buddha's mind, one experiences all thought as the radiance of pure awareness. Sometimes the deities are depicted in their wrathful aspects as demons; these represent negative factors in ourselves that are transformed into positive qualities through practice. Just as the wisdom generated from the mind that perceives emptiness is the foundation for achieving a Buddha's Truth Body, so the method of deity yoga is the foundation for achieving a buddha's Form Body. Deity yoga is termed "yoga with signs," whereas the corresponding meditation on emptiness is termed "yoga without signs."

There are four classes of Tantra: (1) Action Tantra, (2) Performance Tantra, (3) Yoga Tantra, and (4) Highest Yoga Tantra. In all four, the practitioner attempts to transform her/his own body, speech, and mind into their enlightened state by using the visualized deity as a model. The meditator simultaneously visualizes the deities and realizes their empty nature. All four require some form of tantric initiation. *Action Tantra* is so called because it primarily involves external rituals such as making offerings, ritual bathing, and symbolic hand gestures (*mudras*). These activities are used as symbols of the process of purification. At this stage, one may simply imagine the deity in front of oneself, although there is a self-generation practice. In *Performance Tantra* one engages in both internal and external practices and generates oneself as a living embodiment of the deity. Neither action nor performance Tantra requires Tantric vows, but the practitioner must have taken the Bodhisattva vows. However, in order to practice *Yoga Tantra* it is necessary to take the Tantric vows. At this stage, internal practices are emphasized to develop meditative stabilization. *Highest Yoga Tantra* is the culmination of the previous three and presents techniques for aligning the subtlest levels of the mind with the path of the Dharma.

At each stage of Tantra the practitioner works with an increasing level of desire. The practitioner transforms feelings of desire into a state of mind focused on emptiness. This experience is said to generate a feeling of bliss, and if one can unite this bliss with the experience of emptiness, then one is said to be able to eliminate all negative mental states. As the visualizations are actualized in a union of bliss and emptiness, deities of Highest Yoga Tantra are depicted in sexual embrace.

HIGHEST YOGA TANTRA

The Dalai Lama describes Highest Yoga Tantra as the "daily diet" of Tibetan Buddhists. In this form of Tantra one generates an image of the deity with the detail of everyday reality and then one transforms oneself into that image. In the lower Tantras the practitioner works to develop a union of calm abiding and higher insight. In Highest Yoga Tantra the practitioner reaches a stage where concentration meditation or calm abiding *actually produces* higher insight. Meditators at this level learn to enter the kind of consciousness experienced during the process of death—the innate mind of *clear light*—and to transform this experience from a neutral one into a positive one. The Truth Body is achieved through the wisdom that perceives emptiness and the Enjoyment Body and Form Body through deity yoga. Then one enters the *vajra-like* meditation, the final meditation before Buddhahood.

Generation and Completion

Highest Yoga Tantra is divided into two stages, the *generation stage* and the *completion stage*. This is a gradual process of developing and familiarizing oneself with the experience of the absolute nature of mind or the "mind of clear light." During the first stage, the practitioner works with creative visualization to transform their ordinary body, speech, and mind into their wisdom aspects: *vajra body*, *vajra speech*, and *vajra mind*. *Vajra* means "diamond" and refers to the indestructibility and clarity of Buddha-consciousness.

To develop pure perception, all sounds are regarded as mantras and all thoughts as the radiance of pristine awareness.

In order to realize the essential purity of all phenomena, one visualizes oneself and all other sentient beings as wisdom deities and the surrounding world as a mandala. "This is not some artificial idea of purity that you try to superimpose upon phenomena," says Dilgo Khyentse Rinpoche. "It is, rather, the recognition that all phenomena are truly and inherently pure." Tantric practitioners study the qualities of the Bodhisattvas through deity yoga with the attitude that these qualities are presently existing aspects of their own minds. The completion stage is the complete awareness of the ultimate nature of mind. Even subtle obscurations to the "omniscient mind" (the complete simultaneous knowledge of all phenomena), such as the imprints of dualistic appearances are overcome. Through the use of various practices and yogas one is able to generate and control a subtle body called an *illusory body*, and one perceives all phenomena as being the "play" of the radiant mind of clear light.

The sexual imagery of Tantra has captured the imagination of many Westerners looking for something beyond the conventional exploitation of sexual consciousness. However, it is not a practice that one can learn from a book. Without the proper teachings and guidance, it simply will not achieve any significant result. Only very advanced meditators practice with consorts, as it takes a vast understanding and must be entered into without a tinge of self-indulgence. "Truthfully, you can only do such practice if there is no sexual desire whatsoever," says the Dalai Lama. "The kind of realization required is like this: If someone gives you a goblet of wine and a glass of urine, or a plate of wonderful food and a piece of excrement, you must be in such a state that you can eat and drink from all four and it makes no difference to you what they are. Then maybe you can do this practice."

PRELIMINARIES FOR TANTRIC PRACTICE

The texts of the *Lamrim* or "Stages of the Path" set out a number of progressive steps that are prerequisite meditations and contemplations for studying Tantra:

1. Learning from a qualified spiritual master;
2. Contemplating the value and potential of this human life;
3. Meditating upon the inevitability of one's own death and the impermanence of all phenomena;
4. Contemplating the sufferings of beings in other realities;
5. Meditating upon the karmic law of cause and effect;
6. Generating dissatisfaction with the repetitive cycles of existence;
7. Developing confidence in the Buddhas, the teachings, and the spiritual community (the Three Jewels);
8. Developing the ability to see all things as equal;
9. Learning to view all sentient beings as if they were one's mother or closest friends;

10. Remembering the kindness of others;

11. Recognizing the equality of oneself and others;

12. Meditating on the disadvantages of cherishing oneself;

13. Meditating on the advantages of cherishing others;

14. Exchanging oneself with others (*Tonglen*);

15. Developing great compassion;

16. Taking responsibility to relieve the suffering of others;

17. Sharing one's benefits and merits with others;

18. Developing Bodhicitta (the mind of Enlightenment that seeks to eliminate all suffering);

19. Developing concentration through advanced meditational practices;

20. Developing the wisdom that perceives the truth of emptiness.

Apart from engaging in the practice of the Six Perfections, the five formal preliminary practices are: (1) taking Refuge, (2) prostration, (3) Vajrasattva meditation, (4) mandala offering, and (5) Guru Yoga.

1. Taking Refuge

Taking Refuge is establishing a profound trust based on investigation in the power and efficacy of the Three Jewels (the Buddha, the Dharma, and the Sangha) to relieve suffering (see Chapter 7).

2. Prostration

Prostration is a purification practice that is used as a tool to transcend the personal ego and overcome arrogance. The practitioner begins by standing with legs together. The base of the palm and the tips of the fingers are pressed together and point upward, making a space in the middle that the thumbs are tucked into. The practitioner raises the hands a couple of inches above the head, and with the hands still pointing upward, touches the top of the head, the throat, and the heart. These symbolize the three doors: the body, speech, and mind of a buddha; touching each of these places symbolizes one's wish to attain these qualities in oneself. The practitioner then kneels down and places the forehead on the floor and the palms flat on either side. S/he then stands, brings the palms together overhead, and the process is repeated.

In a full prostration, instead of kneeling, the whole body is laid flat out on the floor and the arms are stretched above the head before rising. One imagines the Buddhas and Bodhisattvas all around. One acknowledges their superior compassion and wisdom and, at the same time, aligns oneself with one's own potential for attaining their state of Enlightenment. In order to enter into Tantric practice a practitioner is generally required to carry out one hundred thousand prostrations. Westerners often misunderstand prostrations to be an act of personal obeisance, but when Buddhist students prostrate before their teacher they are not bowing to the teacher's personality, but to what s/he represents—Buddhahood itself. Teachers in turn prostrate before they give teachings and before their own gurus for the same reasons.

3. Vajrasattva Meditation

Vajrasattva is a Buddha who represents the purified mind. His name means "Spiritual Hero of Indestructible Reality." This practice usually requires a Vajrasattva empowerment. You visualize a throne, on the seat of which is a lotus flower. On the flower are two circular cushions: the bottom one is a moon disc, and the top one is a sun disc. Upon them is the syllable **HUM**. This **HUM** turns into Vajrasattva, and the **HUM** syllable rests at his heart. His body is a brilliant white, and he is sitting in a half-lotus position. The toe of his right foot gently touches the top of your head. His right hand is close to his heart and holds a golden *dorje*, a scepter-like object sometimes called a vajra. His left hand is at his left hip and holds a bell, turned slightly upward so that you can see the hollow space inside. The vajra symbolizes *skillful means* or the enlightened method of love, compassion and bodhicitta, and the bell symbolizes the *wisdom* that understands emptiness.

Vajrasattva's one-hundred syllable mantra surrounds him from left to right, the short version of which is **OM VAJRASATTVA HUM.** The **HUM** syllable radiates light all around, a light that travels through space and eliminates the ignorance of sentient beings everywhere. Then you confide to Vajrasattva all the things you regret having done, said, and thought, and you resolve not to engage in these actions again. As you say the mantra, you visualize Vajrasattva's wisdom and compassion as a stream of nectar emanating from his heart and flowing through him into your body from the top of your head. This light purifies all negative emotions and negative karma that is emitted from your pores, palms of your hands, and soles of your feet. This negativity is replaced by healing nectar that fills your body with a sense of well-being. You feel that you have actually been transformed into Vajrasattva, with all his wonderful qualities of body, speech, and mind.

4. Mandala Offering

All four Tantras require the use of a mandala. The Sanskrit word *mandala* means "extracting the essence," whereas the Tibetan translation suggests "wholeness" or "circumference." A mandala offers a conceptual framework for one's meditation, and in Tibetan Buddhism it represents the enlightened state. It is a sacred environment, a Pure Land in which the perfected qualities of a particular Buddha are represented. Mandalas are used as a meditation tool to align the microcosm with the macrocosm—the conventional mind with the mind of Enlightenment. The *outer mandala offering* utilizes material images and the practitioner offers the entire universe through this image to the Three Jewels of Buddha, Dharma, and Sangha. The Dalai Lama says that this symbolizes "the overcoming of even a subtle form of possessiveness and attachment." The *inner mandala offering* practice takes place in the mind, during which one offers one's own physical existence, visualizing parts of the body as parts of the universe.

Mandalas are images that represent specific Buddhas and the perfected state that one is attempting to realize in oneself. They can be made from cloth or colored sand or be generated from the meditator's own imagination. They usually include concentric circles bounded by a square within an outer circle. The square has an opening on each side, symbolizing the doors to the Buddha's palace. This is the central focus of the meditation, representing the creation of the deity's enlightened mind.

Outer Mandala Meditation

You will need a round plate about eight inches in diameter. Regardless of what it's made from, it should be visualized as pure gold, symbolizing one's pure Buddha-nature. For offerings you can use small grains, rice, colored sand, or precious stones. The following example uses grain as the offering:

1. Hold the plate at heart level with your left hand.
2. Drop some grain from the right hand onto the center of the plate while generating Bodhicitta and reciting the refuge prayer.

I take refuge in the Buddha, I take refuge in the Dharma,
I take refuge in the Sangha.

Sanskrit: *Namo Buddhaya, Namo Dharmaya, Namo Sanghaya*

3. Using the right forearm, you then wipe the grain off the plate in a clockwise motion three times. This symbolizes the wiping out of desire, hatred, and ignorance.

4. Drop some more grain on the plate and wipe it three times in a counterclockwise direction. This symbolizes the aspiration to develop positive qualities of body, speech, and mind.

Next stage:

1. Let the grain pour slowly from the right hand to make a circle around the center of the plate.

2. Form a hill of grain in the center of this circle. This symbolizes Mount Meru, the symbolic center of the universe.

3. At each of the four points of the compass make four piles of grain, symbolic of the four main continents of the primordial universe.

4. Make two more piles on either side of the central one, symbolizing the sun and the moon.

5. One should bring to mind the vastness of the entire universe and should offer it up to the buddhas in order that all sentient beings within it can receive their qualities.

6. Tip the plate toward yourself and pour the grain onto your lap. This symbolizes the blessings you and all beings in the universe receive from making these offerings. If you are making requests, tip the plate towards an image of the guru (either actual or mental).

Inner Mandala Offering

Here, one's own body becomes the mandala. This is a practice that helps to purge negative attitudes toward the body. You imagine that your skin and hair is pure gold, your blood is nectar, and your flesh is beautiful heavenly flowers. The trunk of your body is Mount Meru, the center of the universe, and is made of precious stones and metals. Your arms and legs are the four continents and the fingers and toes are smaller lands. Your head is the abode of the Lord of Deities who resides at the peak of Mount Meru, and your eyes are the sun and the moon. Your heart is seen as the most wondrous gem in the universe and the other organs are seen as stores of treasure. Then the whole mandala, seen as a Pure Land, is offered to the Three Jewels (Buddha, Dharma, Sangha) and you receive the blessings of all the enlightened beings.

The *secret mandala offering* is found in highest yoga tantra. Here, the mandala is the mind of Enlightenment itself. This is a more difficult and subtle practice where one transforms the mind into the bodies of a Buddha.

5. Guru Yoga

Pabongka Rinpoche describes Guru Yoga as "the very life-blood of the Tantric path." The meaning of *Guru Yoga* is "uniting with the teacher's nature." It involves practices in which one meditates upon one's spiritual mentor as a living Buddha. This practice instills in the student the possibility of attaining Buddhahood in human form and the teacher becomes a template for the student's spiritual aspirations. By having a human model of Enlightenment the practitioner can more easily identify with and develop enlightened qualities within her/himself. Westerners are suspicious of hierarchy. However, as Lama Edward Kanga Vassel explains, an authentic lama never places her/himself above anyone but allows her/himself to be used as an object of Refuge. "We might be completely unable to get beyond our perception of the lama as being human just like us....At the other extreme a naive deification of the lama may result in a kind of emotionally dominated delusional state that exaggerates our vulnerability to our own personal weaknesses and those of others."

No teachers are entirely free of imperfections, but the point of guru yoga is to learn to see perfection incarnate. As John Powers writes, "Those who critically focus on the guru's faults remain trapped by the ordinary." However, it is important that the student rely upon a fully qualified spiritual guide. Pabongka Rinpoche says that at the very least the guru should have a mind pacified by ethics, concentration and wisdom and possess the qualities of love, compassion, and realization into emptiness. Through Guru Yoga, Enlightenment becomes a more tangible reality, accessible through a living breathing being, and not merely through disincarnate entities. Ultimately, the practitioner comes to see that there is no fundamental difference between the meditational deities, the guru, and the student.

MANTRAS

Mantras are used so extensively in Tantric practice that Tantra is sometimes referred to as Mantrayana, or "Mantra Vehicle." The word mantra means "that which protects the mind," and what the mind is being protected from is ordinary perception. A mantra is a chant or prayer that stills and focuses the mind by turning its tendency to babble with thoughts into a positive quality. A mantra can be either spoken quietly or repeated mentally. Instead of voicing ordinary thoughts and concerns, the mind learns to speak with the voices of the Buddhas as each Buddha has its own mantra. Mantras are the manifestation of enlightened sound, and when a practitioner recites them with the correct attitude and concentration they have the power to invoke the Buddha-nature within.

Many mantras are more or less meaningless when translated literally. They are holographic and holistic cosmic messages, in that each part contains the essence of the whole and can be seen in numerous fields of context. Kalu Rinpoche states that mantras are the union of sound and emptiness. A mantra "has no intrinsic reality, but is simply the manifestation of pure sound, experienced simultaneously with its emptiness." Thus our speech becomes transformed into awareness.

OM MANI PADME HUM—The Mantra of Compassion

The sounds of wind and running rivers,
the crackling of fire, the cries of animals,
the songs of birds, human voices—all
the sounds of the universe—are the vibration
of the six-syllable mantra.

—DILGO KHYENTSE RINPOCHE

The deity Avalokiteshvara, who in Tibet is known as Chenrezig, is the Buddha of compassion, representing the collective love and compassion of all the Buddhas and Bodhisattvas. Avalokiteshvara is regarded as the karmic deity of Tibet (the nearest Western equivalent of which would be a patron saint). All the Dalai Lamas of Tibet are regarded as incarnations of Chenrezig. His mantra is OM MANI PADME HUM, which Tibetans pronounce OM MANI PEME HUNG. Known as the *mani,* this mantra is considered to be the most powerful of all. There is an old saying in Tibet that any child who can say the word *mother* can also repeat the mani. This mantra is said to condense within its six syllables all of the Buddha's teachings: OM being the essence of enlightened form, MANI PADME being the essence of enlightened speech, and HUNG being the essence of enlightened mind. The six syllables of the mani are also related to the six perfections.

Dilgo Khyentse Rinpoche writes, "It is said that a Buddha is capable of extraordinary feats beyond the capacity of any other being…but that even he would not be able to fully describe the merit generated by a single recitation of the mani. Were he to so much as begin such a description, even if all the forests on earth were made into paper, there would never be enough to write down more than the minutest part." OM MANI PADME HUM can be loosely translated as "Praise to The Jewel in the Lotus," the jewel being universal compassion. The lotus is a flower that is born from mud and yet rises above it unsullied, symbolizing the pure path to Buddhahood from the realm of samsara.

INITIATION

Just as taking the Bodhicitta vow is the doorway to the bod-hisattva path, so partaking in initiation is the door to the path of tantra. Such initiations must be received from a qualified teacher. The initiations in Action Tantra, Performance Tantra, and Yoga Tantra are quite similar, but those for Highest Yoga Tantra vary considerably. There are many kinds of initiations and different schools use different names to describe them.

Generally there are four types: (1) vase initiation, (2) secret initiation, (3) wisdom-knowledge initiation, and (4) word initiation. All four initiations are required in Highest Yoga Tantra.

The *vase initiation* enables a practitioner to practice the generation stage. The *secret initiation* allows the practitioner to practice in developing the subtle body. The *wisdom-knowledge initiation* allows a practitioner to meditate on the innate mind of clear light, while the *word initiation* enables meditative practices on the union of the bliss and emptiness. Even when one receives an empowerment from a teacher, one may take the empowerment again and again, both formally and in one's own meditations (if one has completed the standard practices of the deity), in order to restore the transgressed vows and commitments and also to continue to increase one's spiritual understanding.

Death and Dying

Stripped of a physical body, mind stands naked,
revealed startingly for what it has always been:
the architect of our reality.

—SOGYAL RINPOCHE

Death and dying is a subject that is treated very differently in Tibet than it is in the West. Death is a popular topic in all Buddhist teachings, and in fact, the Dalai Lama has said that all his meditations are, ultimately, a preparation for death. Buddhists are not only encouraged to contemplate their finite existence, but to analyze deeply and even to rehearse for the moment of death. Practitioners are taught to imagine various scenarios for their own deaths in their meditation practices and to explore the thoughts and feelings that arise, so that at the time of death they will be mentally and emotionally prepared.

Tibetans do not celebrate the birthdays of their great masters but their death-days, the time that they reached the highest realization—the final Nirvana. For a Buddhist master, death is the pinnacle of their spiritual practice and an unparalleled opportunity for liberation. Death should not be feared, but neither should it be taken lightly. For the spiritually unprepared, death can be an overwhelmingly terrifying experience, but if one has become familiar with deeper states of mind during one's life, then death can be an opportunity for spiritual liberation. The process of dying is one of letting go of attachments. For someone still clinging on to life, this will mean a painful process of having the things and people they love pried out of their grasp. If the dying person is calm and unafraid, then the letting go process does not have to be forced on her/him; s/he can participate in it willingly and consciously.

The two things that matter the most at the time of death are the kind of life one has led and the present state of one's mind. The karmic imprints of one's life directly determine one's next rebirth, and the final thought or emotion before death will exert a profound influence upon one's experience in the after-death states. It is because of this that a peaceful and supportive environment at the time of death is considered by Buddhists to be of the utmost importance.

THE BARDOS

For Tibetan Buddhists, consciousness does not die with the body but continues in subtle form in metaphysical dimensions of being called *bardo* states. The word bardo means "transition" and also "hanging in between." Therefore, a bardo is an interval between two things. A temporal bardo is a period of time, such as the period between sunrise and sunset. A spatial bardo is the space between things, such the space between two houses. A bardo can also be the interval between thoughts, an interval that meditators learn to expand. In fact, one's entire experience is filled with these spaces. On the macro level, however, bardos are the transitions of life, death, and beyond, experienced by every being in samsara—even insects.

Bardos are opportunities, periods when there is an added potency to events and extra potential for awakening to the ultimate nature of reality. The subject of the bardos has been intricately developed in the literature of the Vajrayana tradition, particularly within the Nyingma and Kagyu schools. The most famous text is *The Tibetan Book of the Dead*, which outlines in detail the various stages of death. This text was said to have been hidden by Padmasambhava in the eighth century and lay undiscovered for six hundred years. There are six bardos which span life, death, and after death.

The bardos of life are:

1. The bardo of gestation. This period begins at the end of the bardo of becoming and lasts until the time of physical birth.

2. The bardo between birth and death, including the moment of death. Within the bardo between birth and death are two other bardos:

3. The bardo of the dream state.

4. The bardo of meditative stability. For one very adept in meditation, this is the interval between the experience of deep meditative states and one's return to worldly activities.

The bardos of death are:

5. The bardo that occurs in between the blackout of consciousness after death and the awakening of consciousness three-and-a-half days later. It is said that disturbing the body during this stage risks interfering with this process and has led to the tradition in Tibet of not moving the body of a dead person for this period of time.

6. The bardo of becoming is the period between the re-awakening of consciousness and the unification of that consciousness with the sperm and the egg. Generally, the term bardo is used in reference to this phase.

To give the practitioner some sense of the difficulty of retaining consciousness during these states, the bardo between birth and death is compared to our waking state, the bardo of blackout consciousness after death is compared to going to sleep, and the dream state is compared to the bardo of becoming. Very few people have developed sufficient sensitivity to notice the state immediately after falling asleep and before dreams begin, and the difficulty of remaining conscious after death is even greater than gaining conscious control of our dream state. However, it is said to be possible to experience all the bardo states within our lifetime, as advanced yogic masters are able to simulate the process of death.

It is during this present life bardo that we have most opportunity for development. The practitioner is encouraged to view all experiences in the bardos after death as projections of her/his own mind, but if s/he has not developed this ability in life it will be almost impossible to do so when s/he dies. It is said that however difficult it seems to calm the mind during life, it is much more difficult at the time of death.

PHOWA—Transference of Consciousness

Phowa is a meditation practice that has been used in Tibet for centuries to help the dying. It involves transferring one's mind, or the mind of another person into an enlightened consciousness at the moment of death. The Buddha Amitabha, the Buddha of Limitless Light, is often invoked, as it is this Buddha who embodies the luminosity that the mind experiences at the moment of death. This abbreviated and simplified version of the practice, described by Sogyal Rinpoche, can be done for someone who is dying or even for a person who has already passed away. It can also be done for oneself.

Essentially the Phowa practice is a meditation whereby one visualizes the person merging with the mind of the Buddha or other divinity. Phowa for oneself involves merging one's mind with a Buddha one feels a close connection with, either by visualizing a Buddha in front of oneself or by simply merging one's mind with the deity. One then asks for forgiveness for past negative actions, and for a peaceful death that will benefit other beings. Phowa for a dying person or for someone who has already died requires visualizing a Buddha above the person's head. One next imagines light rays pouring from this Buddha's presence and into that person's mind, purifying them completely. Then one imagines that the dying or dead person dissolves into light and merges with the essence of the spiritual being. The full Phowa practice is a much more complex ritual involving meticulous timing and should be done only by a qualified master or by a qualified Phowa practitioner for herself before death.

THE STAGES OF DEATH

The moment of death holds a powerful spiritual opportunity for every being. Even if one has not lived a very productive or positive life, the time of death still harbors potential for purification for those with the right mindset. The dying process is described in terms of two phases: the "outer dissolution" of the sense powers and the "inner dissolution" of the mental states.

The first thing that happens is that one's senses stop functioning, and then the elements that supported one's physical existence begin to dissolve. A dying person experiences a heaviness and weakness that is associated with the dissolution of the earth element. The dissolution of the water element is when the dying person loses control of the body fluids. The dissolution of the fire element is associated with the loss of bodily warmth, and the dissolution of the air element is signaled when the dying person begins to have difficulty breathing.

The inner dissolution begins with the manifestation of the "ground luminosity" or "clear light." This is actually the revelation of our own fundamental nature, which is also the fundamental nature of all phenomena. Liberation can occur at this moment if the dying person is able to recognize the clear light as the foundation of her/his own wisdom mind and unite with it. Says Sogyal Rinpoche, "When the Ground Luminosity dawns, the crucial issue will be how much we have been able to rest in the nature of mind, how much we have been able to unite our absolute nature and our everyday life, and how much we have been able to purify our ordinary condition into the state of primordial purity." If the dying person recognizes the clear light for what it really is, it is said that s/he will respond to it as naturally as a child running into its mother's arms.

If the clear light goes unrecognized, then the mind enters the bardo of the blackout stage, a period of unconsciousness that lasts about three-and-a-half days. When the consciousness awakens, the true and uninhibited mind unfolds like a flower, exhibiting its natural radiance, which is experienced as color, light, and sound. This energy then coheres to form a mandala of peaceful and wrathful deities. Once again, if the person can recognize that the mind which perceives the deities and the deities themselves are fundamentally the same, then Liberation can occur. "As long as we have no direct realization, however," states Kalu Rinpoche, "the mind has the impression of being an 'I' which experiences and takes as 'other' that which is experienced." Although the manner in which these deities appear may differ depending upon one's conditioning, the experience itself is said to be inherent in all beings.

If the mind still does not recognize itself, the consciousness then enters the phantasmagoric bardo of becoming. Here the mind takes on a mental body in a dimension where thoughts literally form one's reality. In this bardo, the mind has the power of all the senses of the physical body, but with the ability to pass through solid objects, the power of teleportation, and some rudimentary telepathic abilities. Yet, in the bardo of becoming, one is still merely an automaton, programmed by one's karmic past.

All kinds of visions and experiences can be had in this bardo, which can last up to forty-nine days. In Tibet, the custom developed of having lamas do prayers and empowerments for the deceased during this period, in the belief that the benefits of such practices would reach the deceased's consciousness. Again, if one can recognize the nature of one's mind in this bardo, then there is still the possibility for Enlightenment, but at this stage it is extremely hard for someone who has not trained her/his mind to focus even for an instant. The mind is not under conscious control and flails about restlessly. It is said that many people in this bardo don't even realize they are dead and may try to contact living friends and relatives. Some even get trapped and remain in this dimension as spirits or ghosts. The next stage in the bardo of becoming is that the mind develops a powerful desire for a body and one begins to be drawn toward one of the six realms of rebirth. One sees one's future parents having sex and feels pulled toward them. Even at this stage, it is said to be possible to turn back from rebirth by visualizing the potential parents as Buddhas and by renouncing one's feelings of attachment. Otherwise, one is compelled to enter the womb, and the cycle begins anew.

As Buddhists do not believe in an inherently existing and unchanging soul, it is reasonable to ask what it is that takes rebirth. The Dalai Lama explains that "the consciousness that continues from life to life is a subtle consciousness—the faculty of experiencing and being aware, the natural clarity of the mind." The only thing we take with us from this life is the effect of our actions, our karma. Rather than the Hindu idea that our rebirths are like pearls on a necklace and the soul is like the string that links them, H. W. Schumann describes the Buddhist concept of rebirths as analogous to a stack of books, where the placement of each book is not due to any singular shared connection but to a certain set of causes and conditions. These conditions are our karma, and it is this that forms the continuum for our existence in the cycle of life, death, and rebirth.

The Four Schools

*In the course of time, different lineages
appeared...influenced by extraordinary
masters who, at different times and in different
places, expressed the teachings
in slightly different ways.*

—DALAI LAMA **XIV**

The four schools of Tibetan Buddhism are called Nyingma, Kagyu, Sakya, and Gelug. Although the differences between them are often emphasized, what they share in common is greater than what sets them apart. The Dalai Lama has described the four schools as being like different kinds of airplanes that, in spite of differences in design and manufacture, use the same fuel and serve the same purpose. Within the Tibetan traditions, although there are some basic differences of terminology and custom, all outline a path toward the same goal—Enlightenment.

The basic philosophical perspective is the Middle Way School of Nagarjuna. All schools emphasize the importance of not clinging to the world and to life, and all adhere to the *vinaya*, the monastic code of conduct. Their systems are all inspired by the original Indian texts, and all utilize the teachings of both Sutra and Tantra. All four schools employ aspects of the three vehicles: Hinayana, Mahayana, and Vajrayana, and each school acknowledges the masters of the other schools and often share in their practices. They all agree on the fundamental path to Liberation and on the basic practices. They all begin with the generation of Bodhicitta, the "mind of Enlightenment," and then move on to the Bodhisattva levels and the Six Perfections. The main differences are among the lineages the schools follow and the type of Tantric practices they engage in.

In each of the four schools of Tibetan Buddhism there is a threefold approach to Dharma practice: (1) intellectual study, (2) contemplation, and (3) meditation (direct experience). Although the Gelug and Sakya schools initially emphasize a more intellectual and academic approach, and the Kagyu and Nyingma favor a more intuitive meditative approach, practitioners of all schools study the discourses of the Buddha (Sutras), monastic discipline (Vinaya), and the psychology of the Buddhist tradition (Abhidharma), and all employ the Tantric methods of Vajrayana.

All four schools agree that no mental impurities are intrinsic to the mind and that the true nature of mind is clear light, although their methods of expressing this idea vary slightly. All are in agreement that it is the mind that is responsible for keeping one in the repetitive cycle of samsara and that it is the mind that can free one from this state. Most importantly, each school is said to have the necessary teachings and methods to allow a dedicated practitioner to become a Buddha in a single lifetime.

NYINGMA

Nyingma means "Ancient Translation School," and it is the oldest Buddhist school in Tibet. It was founded by the eighth-century Indian tantric adept, Padmasambhava, who was regarded by Tibetans as a second Buddha. His name means "born from a lotus," for legend says that he emerged from the bud of a lotus flower at birth. He was raised by a king in a palace and, like Shakyamuni Buddha, he rejected the life of luxury to pursue his spiritual ambitions. Padmasambhava went on to learn advanced Tantric practices, receiving a number of his teachings from *Dakinis* (female deities).

It was Padmasambhava who brought Buddhism to Tibet, and many extraordinary legends are associated with him. The king of Tibet, Trisong Detsen, was so impressed with Padmasambhava that he declared Buddhism the national religion. Together they established the first monastery in the country named Samye, where many Buddhist texts were first translated from Sanskrit into Tibetan. Regarding them as being more authentic, the Nyingma school relies on the earliest translations of tantric texts. Three subschools have since developed: the *Mind School*, the *Centeredness School*, and the *Quintessential Instruction School*.

The Nyingma classify its teachings into three main groups: the *Oral*, *Treasures*, and *Visions*. The Oral encompass the tantras and associated texts of the *Mahayoga*, *Anuyoga*, and *Atiyoga*. The Treasures refer to a secret transmission lineage—that of the *termas*. Together with the wisdom dakini, Yeshe Tsogyal, Padmasambhava began the tradition of hiding texts, relics, and ritual implements in sacred sites around Tibet. These termas are like time-capsules of knowledge, for the early masters planned that they would be found by realized adepts at particular times in history when they were needed. The termas are protected from premature discovery by powerful spells watched over by Dakinis. Those who are able to unravel the mystery of their location are Bodhisattvas called *tertons,* a word which means "treasure-finders." "Mind treasures" are termas that are not physically discovered but are revealed through the mind of the terton. It is said that many more termas are yet to be found. Lastly, the Visions are teachings revealed by Nyingma masters from mind to mind.

The Nyingma separate the Buddhist teaching tradition into nine vehicles. The first six—the Hearer, Solitary Realizer, and

Bodhisattva, plus the "three outer Tantras" of Action Tantra, Performance Tantra, and Yoga Tantra—are common to all four schools. The last three, exclusive to the Nyingma, are in the category of Highest Yoga Tantra and include the "three inner tantras" of Mahayoga, Anuyoga, and Atiyoga. Mahayoga emphasizes the *development stage* of tantric practice, Anuyoga emphasizes the *completion stage*, and Atiyoga combines the two. These "inner Tantras" include six Bodhisattva levels not found in other schools. Atiyoga is another name for *Dzogchen*, which means "Great Perfection," a practice considered by Nyingmapas (the followers of the Nyingma school) to be the most profound in all of Buddhism. Dzogchen is the state of awakening to one's own primordial nature, and, as a system of mind training, it dispenses with all visualizations and leads to a direct experience of the mind's clear light. This system works on the premise that ethical discipline and morality will naturally arise from this experience.

The training involves three aspects of view, meditation, and action. Recognizing the primordial mind is the view, stabilizing that view in concentration is meditation, and applying the view to one's everyday life is the action. (Dzogchen masters encourage their students to meditate with eyes wide open rather than half-closed.) Meditation in Dzogchen is simply resting in the view and experiencing pristine awareness between thoughts, called *rigpa*. All thoughts and emotions are regarded as the "self-radiance" or manifestation of the flow of rigpa, which can be used to redirect one's mind to its fundamental nature. This fundamental nature of mind is also the fundamental nature of all phenomena and is called the "ground luminosity." Rigpa or the "path luminosity" is the key to this awareness. In Dzogchen, enlightenment does not have to be a gradual process but can occur quite suddenly. As a result, some people make the mistake of thinking that Dzogchen is an easy path, whereas it actually requires diligent preparation. Meditation, purification practices, and practices aimed at accumulating merit and wisdom are all integral to the path.

These preliminary practices are collectively called *Ngondro*. They begin with contemplations on the unique opportunity of one's human existence, impermanence, karma, and the sufferings of samsara and revolve around the central practice of Guru Yoga. The essential teaching of Dzogchen is transferred directly from the mind of the teacher to the mind of the student. This takes a form of empowerment called *Trekcho* or "cutting through" where the teacher penetrates the student's conceptual mind and exposes her/his own Buddha-nature, an experience that is described as seeing one's face in a mirror for the first time. Then the practitioner engages in extremely subtle exercises called *Togal,* working directly with the mind's "clear light."

KAGYU

Kagyu means "Teaching Lineage," and its adherents uphold that the knowledge of this school has been handed down in a continuous succession of enlightened masters. Kagyu was the first school of Tibetan Buddhism to maintain its lineage through identifying reincarnations. In the twelfth century, the Karma Kagyu order (now one of twelve Kagyu orders) began recognizing reincarnations of highly advanced teachers—the Karmapas. The Karmapas were also the first to formally establish the bodhisattva principle in their teachings. There are two main roots of the Kagyu school: One is from Marpa Chokyi Lodoe (1012–1099), and the other from Khyungpo Nyaljor (978–1079).

Marpa, a translator of Buddhist texts, was a layman with a wife and children. He traveled many times to India and Nepal and received teachings from 108 spiritual masters and adepts, the foremost of whom were Naropa and Maitripa. Naropa received his training from the Indian tantric master Tilopa (988–1069), who is said to have received instruction directly from the Buddha Vajradhara. Marpa returned to Tibet and passed his knowledge on to his main disciple, the poet-yogi Milarepa (1040–1123). Milarepa began life as the son of a wealthy merchant. When he and his mother were forced into poverty by scheming relatives, he learned the art of black magic to gain revenge and caused the deaths of thirty-five people. He became a disciple of Marpa, who set Milarepa extraordinarily arduous tasks to purify his negative karma. Milarepa attained Enlightenment after spending years meditating in a cave—the first Tibetan to become enlightened in a single lifetime.

Milarepa's main disciple was Gampopa (1079–1153). Gampopa combined Milarepa's teachings into a single lineage—Dhagpo Kagyu, and also incorporated the yogic practices of Milarepa with the established teachings of the Kadampa order (founded by Atisha's disciple, Dromdön). Thus the Kagyu tradition is imbued with both lay and monastic influences. The Dhagpo Kagyu tradition inspired four orders—Tselpa Kagyu, Barom Kagyu, Phagtru Kagyu, and Karma Kagyu—all founded by Gampopa's disciples between the middle and the end of the twelfth century. Within the Phagdu Kagyu eight subschools later developed, only three of which survive today: the Drikung Kagyu, Taglang Kagyu, and the Drukpa Kagyu. The second main Kagyu lineage was founded by Khyungpo Nyaljor and is called the Shangpa Kagyu. Khyungpo was trained in Bon and Dzogchen, but seeking to supplement this knowledge, he traveled to India and received instruction from 150 scholars and adepts. His main teachers were Rahulagupta, Sukhasiddha, and Niguma (Naropa's sister), but he also obtained teachings from dakinis.

Kagyu practitioners are known for their intensive retreats, and all Kagyu teachers must have completed a retreat lasting at least three years. The teachings of all Kagyu orders emphasize yogic practice and the practice of *Mahamudra*. Mahamudra is a Sanskrit word meaning "Great Seal" or "Supreme Symbol," and it is a practice that leads to the realization of emptiness and the ultimate nature of the mind. All subschools of Kagyu also utilize the Tantric practices of the Six Yogas of Naropa. These are (1) the yoga of heat, (2) the yoga of the illusory body, (3) dream yoga, (4) the yoga of clear light, (5) the yoga of the intermediate state (bardos), and (6) the yoga of the transference of consciousness (phowa). In the *yoga of heat* one learns to control energy channels in the body. In the *yoga of the illusory body*, one learns to visualize a subtle body. In *dream yoga*, one learns to consciously direct the contents of one's dreams. In the *yoga of clear light*, one understands the absolute nature of mind. In the *yoga of the bardos*, one learns to recognize the nature of mind in the six intermediate states of life and death. In the *yoga of the transference of consciousness*, one learns to transfer one's own consciousness or that of another at the time of death into a realm from which a fortunate rebirth can be attained.

Chod is a meditative technique associated with the Kagyu but which has been adopted by all four schools. It was popularized by the female yogin Machik Lapdron (1055–1143). During the meditation, practitioners visualize their bodies being eaten by demons, who are seen as merely symbols of the negative emotions. Chod means "cutting," as this practice is said to sever attachment to the body and to the sense of a separate identity or self.

SAKYA

Sakya means "Pale Earth." The name came from the first monastery of this school, which was constructed on light gray soil. The monastery was built in 1073 by Konchok Gyelpo, a member of the Khon family, who are said to have descended from celestial beings. It was they who founded and continue to oversee the Sakya lineage. For a number of generations the Khon family was associated with the Nyingma lineage, but when Konchok Gyelpo's older brother, Sherap Tsultrim, saw Nyingmapas practicing tantric rituals in public (behavior that he considered dangerous and inappropriate), he severed the ties between the Khon family and the Nyingma school. He decided that instead of the old translations preferred by the Nyingmapas, the Khon family would subsequently rely on the later translations, and he sent Konchok Gyelpo to study with the translator Drogmi.

Drogmi Shakya Yeshe traveled to India and studied with a number of masters, receiving teachings on *Lamdre*. These meditative practices, unique to the Sakya, are based on the *Hevajra* tantra which became a central tantric text of the Sakya school. Konchok Gyelpo's son, Kunga Nyingpo (1092–1158), is known

as the "Great Sakyapa," as he compiled Sutra and Tantra practices and doctrines into a coherent path. It was said that he
received teachings directly from Manjushri, the Buddha of wisdom, when he was only twelve years old. These four instructions were considered to contain the essence of Buddhism and
became an integral part of Sakya teachings.

If you cling to this life, then you are not
  a dharma practitioner.
If you cling to existence, then you do not have renunciation.
If you are attached to your own interests, then you do not
  have the mind of enlightenment.
If you hold to a position, then you do not have the
  correct view.

The Khon family continued to produce notable scholars
and teachers such as Konchok Gyelpo's second grandson
Sonam Tsenmo (1142–1182), who became a learned scholar at
the age of sixteen. The third grandson, Jetsun Drakpa Gyeltsen
(1147–1216), gave his first Hevajra teachings at the age of
eleven and went on to become the head of the Sakya lineage.
He systemized the practice of Lamdre into four main aspects:
(1) a correct understanding of emptiness, (2) the practice of
meditation, (3) ritual, and (4) the realization of the goal.
Jetsun's main disciple was his nephew, the renowned Sakya
Pandita Kunga Gyeltsen (1182–1251), the "Scholar of the
Sakyas." Sakya Pandita was believed to be an incarnation of

Manjushri and was said to have been extraordinarily beautiful. He was also a brilliant and learned monk who excelled in oral debates on Buddhist doctrine, and when Jetsun Drakpa Gyeltsen died he took over as head of the Sakya.

In 1244, the Mongol prince Godan, grandson of Genghis Khan, summoned the sixty-two-year-old Sakya Pandita to Mongolia to negotiate the surrender of Tibet to the Mongols. Instead, Godan converted to Buddhism and became Sakya Pandita's student. In 1253, after the death of both men, the Mongol emperor Kublai Khan invited Sakya Pandita's nephew, Drogon Chogyal Phagpa, to his court. Kublai Khan was so taken with the monk's spiritual knowledge that he declared Buddhism the state religion of Mongolia and offered Phagpa the rule of Tibet. Phagpa was succeeded by his brother, and the Sakyapas ruled Tibet for over a hundred years. However, when the Mongol empire fell, the power of the Sakyas also subsided.

Lamdre is the core teaching of the Sakyapa. Lamdre emphasizes the indivisibility of samsara and nirvana, which only appear as one or the other due to one's own perceptions. When perception is obstructed one is in samsara, and when one's perceptions are free of obstructions one is in nirvana. These teachings originated with the Indian adept Virupa. Virupa (formally called Dharmapala) was a monk who secretly practiced Tantra in his monastery. Even after twelve years he still felt he had made no headway, until he had a vision of

Hevajra's consort Nairatmya. She told him that he had indeed progressed spiritually and that he was about to enter the Path of Seeing, after which she gave him Tantric initiations. In another twelve years, Virupa achieved the supreme realization of Mahamudra and became a Tantric adept with remarkable powers. Feeling that he no longer had any use for monastic life, he left the monastery and named himself *Virupa*, which means "ugly" or "crude." He traveled all over India converting people to Buddhism and demonstrating his yogic skill.

The Lamdre teachings remained primarily a clandestine oral tradition until the eleventh century, and even today these teachings are given directly from master to student, who takes an oath of secrecy. The teachings are divided into "general teachings" and "initiate teachings," the latter being given only to very advanced students. Lamdre means "path and fruit." The path is the cultivation of method and wisdom, and the fruit is the attainment of Buddhahood. In this system each being is said to have within them an innate wisdom that is beyond all duality. The mind is said to have the quality of radiance with its ultimate nature being emptiness. Everything one perceives is but a reflection of the radiant mind.

The Sakya order emphasizes scholarly training and monasteries offer degrees in Buddhism called *Geshe*, which means "spiritual guide." The primary Geshe degrees are "master of the four teachings," "master of the ten teachings," and "master of extensive learning." The Sakya school of the Kohn lineage produced two additional lineages. The Ngorpa lineage was founded by Ngorchen Kunga Zangpo (1382–1457), and the Tsarpa lineage, known as the "whispered lineage" was founded by Tsarchen Losel Gyatso (1502–1556).

GELUG

Gelug means "Way of Virtue." Sometimes called the Yellow Hats, this school was founded by Tsong Khapa (1357–1419) in the late fourteenth century. The present Dalai Lama belongs to this tradition, which was inspired by the Kadam order of the eleventh-century Indian master, Atisha. Tradition states that as a young boy in a former incarnation, Tsong Khapa met the Buddha and gave him a crystal rosary. The Buddha, in exchange, gave him a conch shell and told his attendant, Ananda, that the boy would be reborn in Tibet where he would found a great monastery and spread the Buddha's teachings. It is said that Padmasambhava also prophesied the coming of Tsong Khapa.

Tsong Khapa, also known among Tibetans simply as Je Rinpoche, was born in Eastern Tibet and took the vows of a novice monk at the age of seven. He was a child prodigy, excelling in everything that he was taught. He became highly skilled in debate and he earned a reputation as a brilliant scholar and philosopher. Tsong Khapa set about to reform

Tibetan Buddhism, which he felt had lost some of its authenticity and regard for the value of moral discipline. The Gelug school began in 1410 with the founding of Ganden Monastery (named after the Tibetan translation of the Sanskrit word *Tushita*, the heavenly realm of the next buddha, Maitreya) where a strict regimen stressing ethical behavior, philosophical debate, and Tantric practice was instituted. Tsong Khapa also developed a system by which monks could engage in the practices of Highest Yoga Tantra without infringing on their monastic vows.

Tsong Khapa is considered by the Gelugpa to be an incarnation of Manjushri, the Buddha of wisdom. It was said that he could communicate with Manjushri and question him on aspects of Buddhist doctrine. Tsong Khapa traveled all over the country studying with over a hundred of the greatest Buddhist masters of all traditions and schools. One of his disciples, Gendun Druba was posthumously recognized as the first Dalai Lama in the late sixteenth century. He founded Tashihlunpo Monastery in 1445 which later became the monastery of the Panchen Lamas, who rank second only to the Dalai Lamas in the Gelug hierarchy.

Tsong Khapa engaged in extensive meditation retreats, the longest of which lasted four years. He had thousands of students, gave frequent lectures, and wrote eighteen volumes on Buddhist doctrine, which combine aspects of Sutra and Tantra. He began writing his most influential works at the age of thirty-two.

The Great Exposition of the Stages of the Path (Lamrim Chenmo) is the principle tool for Buddhist study for the Gelugpa. This work is based on *A Lamp for the Path to Enlightenment*, written by Atisha, which is why the Gelug school is sometimes referred to as the "New Kadampa" order. Tsong Khapa also wrote a companion work on Tantra, entitled *The Great Exposition of Secret Mantra* (Ngakrim Chenmo). He died at the age of sixty while seated in meditation, and witnesses claimed that his body transformed into that of Manjushri.

The Gelugpas traditionally avoided involvement in politics, but in the late sixteenth century they rose to political power when the Mongol chieftain Alta Khan recognized the head of the Gelugpa, Sonam Gyatso (1543–1588), as the third Dalai Lama. This connection created a powerful bond between the two countries. The Mongol leader later established Ngawang Lobsang Gyatso (1617–1682), the Fifth Dalai Lama, as the political and spiritual leader of Tibet, thus confirming the authority of the Gelug school. The Dalai Lamas remained the rulers in Tibet for three hundred years, up until the Chinese invasion when the present Dalai Lama was forced into exile.

The Gelug tradition emphasizes ethics in the context of a monastic lifestyle. As a result, most Gelugpa lamas are monks, and it is rare to find a lay Gelugpa master. Scholarship is regarded as a necessary foundation for the practice of meditation, and Sutra and Tantric teachings are the subject of critical analysis in oral debates. When a monk has completed his initial training course, he may work toward one of the three levels of the degree of *Geshe,* the doctorate of Buddhist philosophy instituted by the Thirteenth Dalai Lama. These are Geshe Dorampa, Geshe Tsogrampa, and the highest degree of Geshe Lharampa. This degree might take up to twenty-five years to complete and is an extremely exacting program, with only a handful of candidates being awarded the Geshe Lharampa degree each year. Geshe degree holders usually then enter a meditative retreat for up to three years to put their knowledge of Buddhist teaching into full-time practice.

The Gelugpa emphasize the "Three Principle Aspects of the Path," that are said to encapsulate the purpose of Buddhism, some understanding of which is considered essential for the practice of Tantra. They are: (1) the renunciation of cyclic existence, (2) the determination to attain enlightenment for the good of all beings, and (3) the proper understanding of emptiness. In the Gelug school the journey to Enlightenment is presented as a series of gradual steps. This system is called Lamrim or "Stages of the Path," a tradition inspired by Atisha. However, Gelug practitioners combine their studies in the Lamrim with Tantric practice and so they work on understanding aspects of both Sutra and Tantra simultaneously.

Glossary

Afflictive emotions Negative mental states that obscure one's true nature. The main afflictive emotions are ignorance, attachment, anger, pride, and jealousy.

Aggregates Five faculties made up of the aggregation of a number of factors that constitute a sentient being. They are form, feeling, perception/discrimination, conditioning (mental) factors, and consciousness.

Arhat A "foe-destroyer." Someone who has achieved Liberation from cyclic existence by overcoming all emotional afflictions and underlying ignorance. The goal of Hinayana practitioners.

Bodhicitta The altruistic "mind of Enlightenment" that aspires to attain Buddhahood for the sake of all other sentient beings.

Bodhisattva An "Enlightenment hero." Someone who has generated Bodhicitta and is on the path to full Buddhahood.

Buddha One who has removed all obstacles and obscurations to Liberation and Knowledge (perfect awareness).

Calm abiding A meditative state in which one's mind focuses single-pointedly on an object of meditation.

Clear light The subtlest level of the mind experienced in deep meditation and at the time of death. Also called "inner radiance" of the mind.

Dakini Lit., "Sky-goer." A female practitioner who has attained high levels of realization or a manifestation of the wisdom mind of a female Tantric deity.

Deity yoga A tantric practice in which the meditator learns to identify with the form and mind of a meditational deity.

Dharma A word that can refer to both the Buddhist path and the result of following the path, but which generally refers to the teachings of Buddhism.

Emptiness The view that no phenomena possesses a separate independent existence.

Enjoyment Body The ideal nonmaterial form of a Buddha, which resides in a Pure Land. Tantric practitioners attempt to cultivate this body in meditation.

Enlightenment A state of mind of total awakening attained through spiritual transformation. It is characterized by freedom from all dissonant emotions (Liberation) and all limits to perfect knowledge (Omniscience).

Five Paths The levels that an aspiring Bodhisattva travels towards complete Enlightenment. They are: (1) the Path of Accumulation, (2) the Path of Preparation, (3) the Path of Seeing, (4) the Path of Meditation and (5) the Path of No More Learning.

Five Poisons The three main afflictive emotions of attachment/desire, anger and ignorance together with pride and jealousy.

Form Body The Emanation Bodies of a Buddha.

Four classes of tantra Action Tantra, Performance Tantra, Yoga Tantra, and Highest Yoga Tantra.

Four Noble Truths The first teaching the Buddha gave after his Enlightenment. They are: (1) the truth of suffering, (2) the truth of the cause of suffering, (3) the truth of the cessation of suffering, and (4) the truth of the path which leads to the cessation of suffering.

Four Powers (1) The power of regret (2) the power of support, (3) the power of the antidote and (4) the power of resolve that are used in the practice of purification.

Four schools Nyingma, Kagyu, Sakya, and Gelug.

Geshe The highest monastic degree in Buddhism, earned through fifteen to twenty-five years of study.

Guru yoga Tantric meditation in which the practitioner views the teacher as a meditational deity.

Hearer A Hinayana adept. Someone who gains Liberation from hearing the Buddha's teachings.

Higher insight The wisdom or penetrative insight one gains from applying analytical meditation to the subject of emptiness.

Hinayana See Individual Vehicle.

Ignorance The source of all afflictive emotions; the mind that doesn't understand the law of karma and the emptiness of phenomena, especially the emptiness of the self.

Individual Vehicle The Buddhist system where individual rather than universal Liberation is the goal of spiritual practice.

Karma The universal law of cause and effect.

Liberation The freedom from afflictive emotions and from the cycle of rebirth.

Mahayana See Universal Vehicle.

Mandala A pictorial or visualized abode of meditational deities representing the environment of the enlightened mind.

Mantra Syllables that are recited in order to transform ordinary sound into enlightened sound.

Nirvana The state of existence in which all suffering has ceased and all delusions have been overcome.

Omniscience A Buddha's perfect wisdom that perceives all phenomena directly, simultaneously, and nondualistically.

Perfection Vehicle The Sutra system of Mahayana emphasizing the path and practices of the Bodhisattva.

Phowa A Tantric practice in which the consciousness of a dying person is transferred to a realm from which s/he can gain a favorable rebirth.

Prostration A physical practice to counteract the ego and invoke the body, speech, and mind of a Buddha. Also used to purify negative physical karma.

Pure Land A realm of existence free from all suffering, created by a Buddha's influence.

Samsara The cycle of death and rebirth characterized by suffering.

Sangha Refers to those who have directly realized emptiness and also to the ordained monastic community.

Selflessness A synonym for emptiness (as in the selflessness of persons and phenomena).

Six Perfections The practices that a Bodhisattva attempts to perfect.

Six Realms The dimensions of existence in samsara populated by hungry ghosts, hell beings, animals, humans, gods, and demigods.

Skillful Means Refers to the method of love, compassion and bodhicitta which a practitioner integrates with the wisdom of emptiness.

Solitary Realizer An adept on the Hinayana path who, in their last life before Liberation, achieves this state largely independent of a Buddha's influence.

Sutra The discourses that the Buddha gave to his disciples after his Enlightenment.

Tantra Advanced meditational practices of Mahayana and their accompanying texts, which claim to be able to lead a practitioner to full Buddhahood in a single lifetime.

Three Jewels The Buddha, Dharma, and Sangha (essentially the teacher, the teachings/realizations, and the spiritual community).

Three Poisons The main afflictive emotions of attachment and desire, anger and ignorance of the true nature of reality.

Tonglen Literally "giving and taking." A mind-training exercise where one gives one's own happiness and takes on the suffering of others.

Tripitaka Literally "three baskets." The divisions of the Buddha's teaching into the Sutras, the Vinaya and the Abhidharma.

Truth Body The nature of the fully enlightened mind of a buddha—nonconceptual and nondual.

Tulku The reincarnation of a high lama.

Twelve Links of Dependent Origination The process by which all beings enter the cycle of existence.

Two Truths The conventional and ultimate truths describe how phenomena possess a relative and absolute nature.

Universal Vehicle The Mahayana path that emphasizes the altruistic motivation for Enlightenment. Includes the Sutra Vehicle, the Perfection Vehicle, and the Tantra Vehicle.

Vajra The indestructible reality of the state of Enlightenment. Also a tantric ritual object which symbolizes the method aspect of this reality.

Wisdom Perceptual acuity. For Bodhisattvas it is the discriminative awareness that understands emptiness.

Bibliography

Chodron, Pema. *The Wisdom of No Escape*. Boston: Shambhala Publications, 1991.

Coleman, Graham. *A Handbook of Tibetan Culture*. Boston: Shambhala Publications, 1994.

Das, Surya. *The Snow Lion's Turquoise Mane*. New York: HarperCollins, 1992.

Govinda, Lama Anagarika. *Foundations of Tibetan Mysticism*. York Beach: Samuel Weiser, Inc., 1969.

Gyatso, Lobsang Ven. *The Four Noble Truths*. New York: Snow Lion Publications, 1994.

Gyatso, Tenzin (Dalai Lama XIV). *A Flash of Lightning in the Dark of Night*. Boston: Shambhala Publications, 1994.

Gyatso, Tenzin (Dalai Lama XIV). *Freedom in Exile*. New York: HarperCollins, 1990.

Gyatso, Tenzin (Dalai Lama XIV). *Kindness, Clarity, and Insight*. New York: Snow Lion Publications, 1984.

Gyatso, Tenzin (Dalai Lama XIV). *Opening the Mind and Generating a Good Heart*. Dharamsala: Library of Tibetan Works and Archives, 1985.

Gyatso, Tenzin (Dalai Lama XIV). *Path to Bliss: A Practical Guide to Stages of Meditation*. New York: Snow Lion Publications, 1991.

Gyatso, Tenzin (Dalai Lama XIV). *The World of Tibetan Buddhism*. Boston: Wisdom Publications, 1995.

Gyatso, Tenzin (Dalai Lama XIV), Tsong Khapa, and Jeffrey
Hopkins. *Tantra in Tibet.* New York: Snow Lion
Publications, 1977.

Gyeltsen, Tsultim Geshe. *Compassion: The Key to Great
Awakening.* Boston: Wisdom Publications, 1997.

Khyentse, Dilgo. *The Heart Treasure of the Enlightened
Ones.* Boston: Shambhala Publications, 1992.

Kohn, Sherab Chodzin. *The Awakened One: A Life of the
Buddha.* Boston: Shambhala Publications, 1994.

Norbu, Dawa. Tibet: *The Road Ahea*d. New Delhi:
HarperCollins, 1997.

Powers, John. *Introduction to Tibetan Buddhism.* New York:
Snow Lion Publications, 1995.

Rabten, Geshe. *Treasury of Dharma.* London: Tharpa
Publications, 1988.

Rabten, Geshe and Geshe Dhargye. *Advice from a Spiritual
Friend.* London: Wisdom Publications, 1977.

Rinpoche, Kalu. *The Dharma.* New York: State University of
New York Press, 1986.

Rinpoche, Pabongka. *Liberation in the Palm of Your Hand.*
Boston: Wisdom Publications, 1991.

Rinpoche, Sogyal. *The Tibetan Book of Living and Dying.*
New York: HarperCollins, 1993.

Shantideva. *A Guide to the Bodhisattva's Way of Life.*
Dharamsala: Library of Tibetan Works and Archives,
1979.

Thurman, Robert. *Essential Tibetan Buddhism.* Edison, N.J.:
Castle Books, 1997.

Trungpa, Chögyam. *The Path is the Goal*. Boston & London: Shambhala, 1995.

Tsongkapa. *The Principle Teachings of Buddhism*. New Jersey: Mayhayara Sutra and Tantra Press, 1988.

Williams, Paul. *Mahayana Buddhism: The Doctrinal Foundations*. London: Routledge, 1989.

Zangpo, Togmey. *The Thirty-Seven Practices of a Bodhisattva*. Dharamsala: Library of Tibetan Works and Archives, 1976.

Index

Hinayana, 30, 33, 107, 108, 178, 196, 197, 198

I

ignorance, 37, 39, 44, 46, 48, 74, 98, 103, 124, 125, 128, 194, 195, 198
illusory body, 153, 185
impermanence, 11, 38, 39, 182
Individual Vehicle, 31, 32, 33, 196
initiation, 165-166

J

jealousy, 44, 46-47, 98, 128, 194, 195
Jetsen Drakpa Gyeltsen, 187, 188
Jewel Embodiment, 62

K

Kagyu, 13, 22, 102, 169, 177, 178, 183-186
Kalu Rinpoche, 55, 103, 110, 111, 145, 164, 174, 196
karma, 39, 51-56, 97, 115, 116, 158, 176, 182, 184, 196, 197
Karmapas, 54
Khon family, 186, 187, 190
Khyungo Nyaljor, 183, 184
Konchok Gyelpo, 186, 187
Kublai Khan, 23, 188
Kunga Nyingpo / Khyungpo Nyaljor, 186

L

Lama Norhla, 108
Lamdre , 186, 187, 188, 189. *See also* Path and Fruit
Lamrim, 146, 154, 193
Lang Darma, 21

Langri Thangpa, 89
Liberation, 31, 32, 43, 50, 108, 114, 128, 129, 173, 174, 178, 194, 195, 196, 197
Lobsang Gyatso, 37, 38, 192

M

Machik Lapdron, 185
Madhyamaka, 17
Mahamudra, 102, 185, 189
Mahayana, 16, 17, 30-34, 61, 81, 82, 83, 85, 93, 107, 108, 109, 116, 126, 133, 144, 145, 178, 196, 197, 198
Mahayoga, 180, 181
Maitripa, 183
mandala , 153, 158, 159, 160, 161, 196
  mandala offering, 155, 158-159, 160, 161
mani, 164, 165
Manjushri, 187, 188, 191, 192
mantra (Mantrayana), 143, 145, 157, 158, 163-165, 196
Marpa, 183, 184
meditation, 59, 108, 115, 119, 130-142, 178, 181, 182, 185, 187, 195
  analytical, 76, 132, 137-142
  concentration, 76, 132, 134-137, 152
  Tonglen, 98-100
merit, 182
Middle Way, 17
Milarepa, 13, 50, 56, 183, 184
mudras, 150

N

Nagarjuna, 17, 49, 60, 64, 112, 126
Naropa, 183, 184

Sukhasiddha, 184
Sutras, 16, 17, 32, 33, 36, 38, 48,
  56, 65, 107, 121, 144, 147, 149,
  178, 187, 192, 193, 197, 198

T
Tantra, Tantrayana, 34, 108, 143,
  178, 181, 187, 188, 191, 192,
  193, 195, 198
Tara, 20
Ten Grounds of the Bodhisattva,
  124
ten negative actions, 115, 120
ten positive actions, 115, 120
terma, 180
Terton, 180
Theravada, 31, 32, 33, 34
Three Jewels, 58, 60, 61, 62, 63,
  109, 133, 154, 155, 159, 161, 198
Three Pillars of the Dharma, 108
Three Poisons, 43
Three Principle Aspects of the Path,
  147
Thurman, Robert, 114, 147
Tilopa, 183
Togal, 182
Togmey Zangpo, 115
Tonglen, 94, 95-97, 98, 155, 198
Trekcho, 182
Tripitaka, 17, 59, 198
Trisong Detsen, 20, 179

Truth Body, 150, 122, 190, 191, 192
Twelve Links of Dependent
  Origination, 48-49, 198
Two Truths, 71-72, 198

U
Universal Vehicle, 34, 196, 198

V
vajra, 70, 152, 157, 198
Vajrasattva, 155, 157, 158
Vajrayana (see Tantra, Tantrayana),
  30, 108, 143, 145, 169, 178. *See
  also* Tantra, Tantrayana
Vantassel, Edward Kunga, 47, 57
Vinaya, 17, 144, 178, 198
Virupa, 188, 189
vows, 191

W
Wheel of Dharma, 16, 40
Wheel of Life, 42-50, 128
Wisdom, 32, 60, 70, 105, 109, 115,
  118, 123, 1224, 149, 150, 155,
  157, 158, 163, 182, 187, 189,
  191, 197, 198

Y
Yama, 43
Yeshe O, 21
Yeshe Tsogyal, 180

BOOKS BY CROSSING PRESS

OTHER BOOKS IN THIS SERIES

Fundamentals of Hawaiian Mysticism

By Charlotte Berney

Evolving in isolation on an island paradise, the mystical practice of Huna has shaped the profound yet elegantly simple Hawaiian character. Charlotte Berney presents Huna Traditions as they apply to words, prayer, gods, the breath, a loving spirit, family ties, nature, and mana.

Paper • ISBN-13: 978-1-58091-026-2

Fundamentals of Jewish Mysticism and Kabbalah

By Ron Feldman

This concise introductory book explains what Kabbalah is and how study of its text and practices enhance the life of the soul and the holiness of the body.

Paper • ISBN-13: 978-1-58091-049-1 / ISBN-10: 1-58091-049-1

RELATED BOOKS

Stumbling Toward Enlightenment

By Geri Larkin

A humorous and honest collection of Buddhist wisdom from a Western beginner's perspective.

Paper • ISBN-13: 978-1-58761-329-6

Available from Crossing Press and Ten Speed Press wherever books are sold.
www.tenspeed.com